Fifteen Hundr

From The Gutter Up

by
Sean O'Shea

Copyright © 2020 Sean O'Shea

ISBN: 9798691508196

All rights reserved, including the right to reproduce this book, or portions thereof in any form. No part of this text may be reproduced, transmitted, downloaded, decompiled, reverse engineered, or stored, in any form or introduced into any information storage and retrieval system, in any form or by any means, whether electronic or mechanical without the express written permission of the author.

Dedication

This book is dedicated to my Mom who I miss dearly and all those I have met along the long the way, who helped and saved me; but especially to my loving and understanding wife Nic who has picked me up from the gutter, literally!

Brief Biography

Sean O'Shea was born in Birmingham in 1969 and spent many years travelling the globe in search of basic employment.

At the age of 49 he retired from the Commercial Insurance Business he co-owned but, on his journey through life, he has taken on many varied vocational roles from a waiter in an Indian Restaurant, running a pub and a door-to-door salesman.

Today, he is happily married with four gorgeous children and currently lives in the West Midlands.

In his spare time, he enjoys playing backgammon, reading and listening to podcasts, stargazing, cinema, cycling and travel.

"Follow your own path and let people talk."

– Dante Alighieri

Prologue

My brain just can't switch off. Most of the time, well pretty much all the time I just look at stuff and the first thing that goes through my mind is "how can I do that better?"

Just out of the starting block and a kind of an hors d'oeuvres or an amuse bouche to my book and for you to get your teeth into, here are some of my ideas.

For example. I look at chewing gum and think why can't they make a 'popping candy' version? I'd definitely try that.

'Double pull ring cans' with half of the can filled with cherry cola and the other side half filled with lemonade (other flavour drinks available).

Drive-through luxury 'fast food and booze' chains. Would you not go to a drive through restaurant with a reduced but delicious menu, that offered you beef brisket or paupiette of seabass in a delicious homemade marinade with triple cooked chips or salad and a bottle of wine for example? I definitely would.

Candy floss – if you saw for sale, would you not try an apple and cinnamon, cola, grape and cherry or rhubarb and custard flavour? I would be tempted.

Sticky tape, now I can't understand why with modern science today no one has created a tape that when torn, the end of the strip has some kind of crystalised polymer that hardens automatically within seconds and is easily located for future use.

But heh, you're only starting on page one and already I could have made you a millionaire! Read the rest of my book to find out who I am and more importantly why I wrote my book as a legacy as a way to keep my memories alive.

Disclaimer- Please do your own research and check before trying to patent any of the above ideas, these are just random off the cuff concepts.

Introduction

This account of my life is factually correct. Certain names and places have been changed to protect those who wish to remain anonymous. Only a handful of people know my full true story, about twelve to be exact, which will make you, number thirteen. Not even my children are aware of my past. Maybe, one day, they will read this book and make up their own minds. However, from the dozen or so people who do know, including my wife, parents, some close family members and friends, everyone has said I should write a full and concise account. "Who knows" they said, "It might be a best seller!" So, bear with me please, as this is my first venture into writing my life in words. They say everyone has at least one book in them and this is mine. Even so, I am more than a little nervous about telling my life story and the reasons will become clear as you read through my book.

I must admit that sometimes truth can be more imaginary than fiction. You might be annoyed with my story, a little frustrated even but I hope I can give you a small fragment of inspiration that, no matter what life throws at you, you can always get up and try again. Just remember though to dust yourself down and try a little harder next time.

Most people think that "TLC" stands for "Tender Loving Care", but I always thought that it could stand for "Thief, Liar & Cheat!" Over my lifetime so far, I have been all three and sometimes, more than once, a combination of these. I have done many things to excess but I do believe that life must be lived – I could not imagine my life as a hermit or as one of those monks who devotes his whole life to celibacy, this is not for me. I just think that would drive me to drink or insanity or both!

I hope that this book might give you a glimpse into my life and it might impart to you some information to help you make up your own mind as to whether I was determined with a positive outlook or simply a lucky guy who just happened to be in the right place at the right time. At the time of writing this book, our global community was pretty much in total lock down with the Coronavirus. It's a very worrying time but I believe that, when everything seems at its most dire and when life is at is darkest, this is when everyone pulls together as one to fight the invisible enemy. I just hope a vaccine becomes available and is found soon so that we can save lives and we can come out of this whole experience a little wiser and a little kinder.

Now you might decide and skip to the end of the book and read the last chapter but, hey, stop a moment, if you want to know how I let a million pounds slip through my fingers and some basic rules of life, then please be my guest on the roller coaster ride through my life and read on. Without wanting to waffle, it's best to kick start and crack on. Looking back at my life, things have always fallen into a certain type of alignment that has resulted in me sitting here writing this book. I hope you enjoy the read but, even if you do not, negative reviews are fine, but please make them witty and funny, "Don't do Vanilla!"

Chapter 1 – Born and Dread!

Most biographies begin either from the birthdate or at a point a few years from birth, but I have always wondered about the actual point of my conception – that very moment when I was created spontaneously in the heat of the moment. I know from what my mother has repeatedly told me that I was not planned and so, I believe, working back those nine months from my birth, I am forced to believe that it was not in some exotic location nor a romantic Lake District retreat (my parents were penniless), more likely it might have been in a dark ginnel in the shadow of the Rotunda, or down a grimy alley alongside a local dance hall with a live band creating the moody background atmosphere! Or, my personal belief, in a cold, single-room occupancy bedsit in the bleakness of a dark, bleary October night, with the moon casting its stare through the partially closed, thin curtains, like some twilight voyeur!

I was born the eldest of three brothers and, just sometimes, I wonder how life would have panned out if I had been born second instead of first. Looking back, it is probably true to say that, in my opinion, I never really ever wanted to be the first born; I don't even really think, as sad as this may sound, I never truly wanted to be the one who won the race for life. I never wanted the responsibility that came with being the eldest but, obviously, I had no choice or say in the matter. The hairs on the back of my neck prickle and stir whenever I hear the Bohemian Rhapsody lyric from Queen,

"I sometimes wish I'd never been born at all."

I have two younger siblings. Michael, who we call Mike, is just 18 months younger than me, in contrast to my youngest brother who is the youngest by some years; Thomas, or Tom, is 10 years my junior. To this day I wonder, if I hadn't won the race for life, what might have become of the little tadpole in second or third place behind me, would he or she have made it to the top and maybe become a successful actor, lawyer, philanthropist or tycoon even; I wonder. Would he or she have done a better job? God only knows.

I was born in the middle of 1969, just sneaking into the latter end of the decade, around the time of the moon landing. We lived in a quiet suburb of Birmingham, called Kings Heath. We were a normal working-class family; we were on general speaking terms with our next-door neighbours but that was as far as it went. If you lived two or more doors down on either side of our house, it was normally just a polite nod. When we were growing up, I always had a close relationship with my two brothers. However, as we grew up and became teenagers, gradually we all drifted apart and went our separate ways in life. It was only while writing this book that it dawned on me that drifting apart was probably because of me.

Tom, the youngest, is by a country mile the brightest and went off to Cambridge University and studied hard. He has become an accomplished author; Tom is academically gifted and determined and I think he observed everything I did in life and did the exact opposite which, with hindsight, was a good technique in how not to fuck things up. I certainly did not lead by example. My middle brother Mike became a Police Officer, while I just bummed around with no real focus, drive, energy, or passion. I was an enigma to myself and to my family, almost a black sheep.

I don't know how Mike got into the police as I had already got into trouble on a few occasions with the law by the time he made his first application. Mainly petty things like drunken vandalism. Once I'd been on an all-day drinking bender and had started early and walked past a Firkins bakery shop just before they were due to close and, for some reason, I did a karate kick at the shop window. The customers in the shop were highly miffed. I was a drunken idiot; I could never handle my drink and never knew when to stop. I thought I was being one of the lads, but I was a fool, an embarrassment to myself and my family. So, I was a little concerned and unsure if the Police background checks would screw up his application; they didn't, and he got accepted to join the police force. I don't quite know what background checks they did on Mike, but they must have been routine and basic ones.

Mom and Dad both held down steady jobs. Dad had come over from Galway in Ireland from a farming background to take up employment in Birmingham. Mom was originally from County Fermanagh in Northern Ireland, then when she was a young girl aged about ten, all her family migrated and took up residence in Alum Rock, Birmingham. Grandad took up employment for a steel company, he was a wise old man who enjoyed telling a good story and playing cards, especially an Irish game of cards called "25".

I loved my Grandad and was his oldest grandchild and godson. He once wrote a letter to a local newspaper, telling them how proud he was of me, I don't really know why he wrote the letter to them, but I still have it to this day and it remains a cherished personal item. He might have seen an ounce of goodness in me, something no one else saw. My Mom used to tell my Dad "He has the Devil in him, I tell you!"

Mom worked as a cashier in the cafeteria of the local geriatric hospital. Life was never easy as we had no luxuries. Both my parents were quite frugal, most of the groceries we bought were from the basic range or display items that were on offer in the local Irish grocers. The biggest perk for being the oldest child was that I always got new clothes and my brothers ended up with mine.

My Dad's working hours as a bus driver were long for a salary that was not generous; however, it did mean that he was guaranteed employment for as long as he held a full driving licence. My Mother only worked part-time as she had to be back home in time to pick us boys up from school. Despite this, we did enjoy some days out as a family to Weston-Super-Mare or, maybe, to the local zoo and we always went on one family holiday a year, back to my Dad's parents farm in Ireland.

Mom always made sure a meal was ready and waiting for Dad when he got home from work and we always sat down once a week around the table for our weekly family Sunday roast. My Mom was no Delia. I don't think she enjoyed cooking. Both Mom and Dad liked their joint of meat cooked between extra well done and cremated, crispy to the point of extinction. We had no say in the matter so, sometimes, me and my brothers could easily break a sweat grinding, gnawing and chewing. It was sometimes a game to try and guess the type of meat we were eating as it was always covered in thick, dark gravy.

My Mother didn't see the funny side or have much dinner table humour, so our guessing games normally had undesired results, either a clip around the ear or a smack to the wrist. Sunday roast dinner was never much of an enjoyable experience. We couldn't leave the dinner table until everyone's plates were clean and had our parent's permission, so inevitably we ended up finishing our food, then sitting, waiting and watching as Mom and Dad both sat, smoked and chatted, using their large dinner plates as ashtrays.

There was definitely a normality about our family life, a lot of routine – it was never dysfunctional but the major issue and problem for me was my relationship with Mother. I can't say I hated her, but it was a belt buckle notch below that. Your relationship with either of your parents is always an important one – as we can see increasingly in modern times – but my Mother never hid the fact that I was neither planned nor wanted. In fact, she had never wanted any children but, deep down, she believed that it was the expected thing to do to have children once you were married. She never shied away from or felt uncomfortable about telling me that I was not wanted and was not planned, she was so matter of fact about it. I don't believe she was being nasty or vindictive in any way, I think she was just being honest.

However, being told this at such a young age was a difficult pill to swallow and I don't really believe my Mother thought it through as to how her comments might have an impact on a young impressionable boy like myself. Now I know that this happens in a lot of families but, in my case, it had a knock-on effect that was to affect the way that I grew up, the way that I behaved and, perhaps, more importantly, the way that I felt about life and my relationships with other people in my life.

I know many families are built upon unplanned pregnancies so, in that way, my family was no different to many others. However, I do think that what made it worse in my case was the fact that I never felt loved by my Mother. We never bonded, we never really developed a close relationship or deep connection at any level. I can never remember when I was growing up my Mother ever telling me that she loved me or asking me how I was or how I got on at school that day.

What had I done that had made her so unhappy? I just felt like an additional product to her marriage and, as money was tight, another mouth to feed. Another aspect of this relationship was that, in those days, there were no scans to tell prospective parents what sex their child was going to be – you took what nature gave you. However, once Mom knew that she was expecting, she had set her heart upon having a girl – another black mark in my Mother's mind then, when I was born. I don't have any baby photographs; I don't think there were any ever taken.

Because of the relationship with my Mother, I grew up never understanding what love was nor expecting it. Indeed, when I look back, I realise now that Mom and Dad never showed any signs of affection towards each other, they were always bickering or arguing and that was how it rubbed off on my brothers and me. Mother always said that her attitude towards us boys was due to her very strict Catholic upbringing in Ireland. As a result of this, I always swore that, if I were ever to have children of my own, I would never be as strict with them as my parents were with us and that I'd love them and show them unconditional love. I promised myself I would tell them I loved them, each and every day.

Unfortunately, I had a difficult childhood which did not help the relationship with my mother. As a child. I suffered from quite a severe pelvic disease that meant I had to make a multitude of weekly visits to the main children's hospital in central Birmingham, on Broad St. This meant that Mother had to spend numerous days and many hours a month taking me to and from hospital as well as waiting around for me. I do not know whether it was just that Mother did not like hospitals, as she worked in one or whether it was the inconvenience and disruption of her everyday life. Whatever the reason, she never made any bones of the fact that she was not happy about it. I am also not sure how, deep down, she felt about the problems and discomfort that I was suffering with my hip. I don't remember her ever asking me if I was in any sort of pain or anything; there was a total lack of compassion. A real emotional disconnection.

Because my Mother never showed me any love or even affection, it resulted in me not being able to learn how to show her much, if any, love in return – I suppose it was a bit of a Mexican stand-off, not helped by the fact that we both had quite stubborn personalities. In fairness to my Mother, I do believe that, deep down, she did love us three boys, but she just did not know how to show it. She would prefer to use discipline instead of discussion.

When I questioned her about her apathy years later, she said, when she was growing up, she was never shown any love or affection by her parents. Mom told me that, when she was young, she was one of the oldest and it was her duty to help with household chores around the farm. She said she would have been around six years old and was told to clean out the chicken coop when collecting eggs in the morning, all without thanks, it was just the done thing.

When I would turn to her after some argument or showdown, I would ask her "What have I done wrong, why don't you love me?" She would just reply, "It's not you

Sean, it's just how I was brought up." Despite her attempts at reassurance, I took it very badly as I was the oldest and so never developed any rapport with my mother. Because of this constant atmosphere, I was always glad that, as I grew older, I could get out of the house more and join in other groups and activities. In this way, I was able to reduce the openly awkward friction between the two of us.

As a child, I was quite tubby. I would be classed as obese today and this used to upset me. I remember that when I was quite young - I must have been about seven or eight years old – each night when I went to bed I used to have a night time ritual of putting a belt around my waist and pulling it as tight as I could in the sad hope that, if I slept with it on all night, I might wake up thinner. It hurt like hell as the belt was so tightly wound around my stomach, it normally left large red welts which mercifully no one ever saw.

I remember this vividly as I hated the shape of my body, a feeling that was made worse by my primary school classmates, who used to call me "Mr Piggy!" I never realised just how cruel children can be – it hit me hard and affected my self-esteem tremendously and this was possibly something that affected the way that I behaved as I grew older. I know that I couldn't help the way that I looked, I hated my porcine face and body shape, but it was a feeling that was exacerbated by the fact that both my two brothers grew up slim and were good-looking guys.

While I didn't resent them for it, I kept asking myself "Why do I always get the shit genes?" I remember purposely abstaining from food to try and starve my body. I was delusional but, at a young age, it was a ridiculous thing to do as it is at the time when your body needs all the right nutrients while it is growing. However, at that stage in my life, I was a totally messed-up kid and today, I like to think that, as I have grown older, I have matured and learned the true respect I have for myself. I'm not going to say I was an ugly duckling that blossomed and grew up to become a good-looking suave guy with charisma and bags of personality and the muscles to boot; that might happen in a book, it just didn't happen to me. That's just how my body looks, I have always been naturally chubby. I remember overhearing my aunty once telling my mom, "It's just puppy fat, he'll lose it soon." I felt self-conscious but kept my feelings and thoughts to myself.

It is interesting to look at my two brothers. I would say that I had zero common sense, but I had ability, potential and some intelligence. My second brother, who is 18 months younger than me, had zero intellectual ability (he would admit this to me), he has never read a book in his life but has an obscene amount of common sense and he has become a "blues & twos" police officer - with a licence to taser! My youngest brother has an abundance of both intellect and common sense, he has some sort of genius superpower and has become a lecturer and author with a prestigious fellowship at Cambridge University and is very well respected amongst his peers.

He has done very well but, as I have found out, often to my detriment, you can only play the cards that you have been dealt. I never had a path to follow when I was growing up and did not have any ambition to do anything, no passion, drive or dreams to fulfil, whereas both my brothers had aspirations to achieve something.

Looking back at our childhood and as we grew up, we got the basics of our upbringing from Mom, but it was Dad to whom we went if we had a problem, he was always approachable. He was the one who gave us the love and affection and who played games with us. I don't remember ever playing any games with Mom; she was the one who disciplined us, taught us to do chores around the house, she cooked for us and cleaned for us, the one who made sure that we always had clean clothes and polished shoes in which we went to school each day. Dad had all the other responsibilities – we always had food on the table, new clothes and a main holiday each year which, to be fair, was the norm back in the 1980s for families such as ours on our income and budget.

Mom was the one that we all feared. She was a strict disciplinarian and dealt out corporal punishment regularly to at least one of us but, mainly, it was to me as I was the oldest and in her opinion I should have known better. To be fair to her, she had grown up in a harsh climate in Ireland where discipline was rigidly applied and adhered to, and I think that she would have found it hard to adjust to any different way of life. On top of this, I think that having to hold down a job, then wash, clean and cook for three growing boys as well as a hardworking husband, was just too much for her. She always tried her best and I wouldn't criticise her too harshly for the way that she brought us up, but personally because I never got on well with her, life in her house was always hard and stressful as you never knew when she was next likely to rant, shout or scream. With hindsight, her outbursts in many cases were probably justified but, as a youngster growing up, it was hard to understand what was going on. I was like "Mom why are you screaming at me when I'm just playing pillow fights with my brother, or I'm just digging holes in the back garden, or I'm just rearranging my bedroom into a big den?" Now it all makes more sense and I totally understand her constant bad mood. In addition, because Dad was working long shifts on the buses putting in as much overtime as possible, he was not usually around when Mother was having one of her meltdown moments.

As I mentioned, I never felt any love from my mother and she never once told me that she loved me. I never resented her for this as, at the time, I never knew any other form of relationship. As I grew older, it was only then I began to understand and appreciate my Mother, although we never really got on well growing up; it was not until I was in my late thirties that I really managed to build a close bond and connection with her. Finally, after thirty-five years of indifference, of fighting, of shouting, we forgave each other and put our past behind us and we grew to love each other after a late, late start. I knew then that she had always loved me, but that she had difficulty connecting and showing it. We wiped the slate clean over a cup of tea and some chocolate digestives and hugged it out. As we both aged, our love for each other rekindled from an ember, then from a flame to a fire. It took many, many years but we finally got there.

As a young boy, my Mom used to try and teach us all good behaviour and she tried to instil into all three of us a good moral fibre. She would always say to us "If you are going to do something, make sure that you do it well and to the best of your ability." She was a great advocate in the work ethos 'if a job is worth doing then it is worth doing properly'. She always expected us to help around the home; I was doing regular household chores by the age of eight.

Mom made us clean up after ourselves, doing such household duties as hoovering the carpets, washing and drying the dishes, plus other tasks, before we could go out to play. I suppose, upon reflection, this was her way of building good character from an early age. She always said that "this is my house and when you are in it, you live by my standards, my rules." If she thought that we were slipping in this respect, she was not above taking the belt to us – in most cases, I got the belting as I was the oldest and was expected to know better. In my eyes, however, I was merely a young boy trying hard to learn what was right and what was wrong and, frequently, having to find out the hard way.

I remember once my brother did something that was going to get him into trouble and my mother saying angrily "What's happened here? Who's done that?" I think my brother had dropped a plate when doing the dishes or something like that and rather than him take the blame or punishment I quickly swapped places with him and gave him the washing-up gloves whilst I had the drying towel standing over the broken plate. I would take the responsibility for it because I did not want the punishment to be dished out to my younger brother, I would be the one who would take the belt. I'd just rather it was me rather than my kid brother Mikey.

One specific occasion that I recall demanded that I receive a spanking. While Mom was getting the belt, I ran around the side of the bed and, instead of her demanding that I take off my trousers or shorts, I simply adopted the prone position over the bed and pulling my trousers and pants down ready to receive my punishment. To my absolute amazement, for once she found this auto response quite funny and chortled out loud, she found it amusing and I think mellowed her anger. On this occasion, I avoided a belting but it made me realise that, if I wanted to lead a more peaceful life with my mother, then I needed to get on her warmer, less frosty side and to try and make her smile, rather than irritating her. I had to defrost the ice queen!

As I mentioned, I always swore that if I were ever to have children, I would never reprimand them by smacking them or taking the belt to them but, instead, I would try to reason with them as equals. Looking back on the situation now, I think that, certainly for the first 18 months of my life, Mom felt like a single parent, with an unwanted child – especially a male one when all along she had wanted a girl. I don't blame my Mother after all, she had had it hard. I think that she had had a far harder life than Dad, despite coming from similar rural Irish families.

Dad was in an awkward position. On the negative side, he had a tiring hard-working life, driving long routes on the buses and would come home shattered, all too often to walk straight into a strong litany of everything we boys had done wrong. On the positive side, Mother always made sure that he had a hot meal on the table waiting for him when he got home, although I do not ever remember her ever playing with any of us, she was less fun and more functional. While Dad never got involved in the day to day aspects of our life, he always paid all the bills and would take us on day trips to Weston-super-Mare. He generally got off light in terms of household duties, but he always found time to play cards with us and tell us stories about life as he was growing up on a farm in Southern Ireland, digging turf and making haystacks amongst other things.

In that way, I suppose, Mom and Dad complemented each other in terms of parenting skills. I always got on extremely well with my Dad, he really is a true gentleman and, even today, we still do get on well. Despite his long working days, Dad always managed to find time for us when he came home, no matter how tired he was. We always used to look forward to that special time with him.

My Dad has this really special ability of talking to you as if you are the only person that matters or exists; when he talks to you, he gives you 100% of his attention, focus and time which I always felt was a fantastic character trait. He is like this with everyone. It's lovely to watch. With our Mother, it was different. I do not believe that she was truly cut out to be a mother, certainly not of three very different boys with all differing demands and requests but I know she did her best for us throughout her life.

At the time, when I would have been about nine or ten years old, I used to play a lot of games by myself in my bedroom. In my little sanctuary I wasn't being taunted by my schoolmates about being chubby, I wasn't being hounded by my mother and so, I enjoyed the solitude of my little room, I could live in my own little world. Having said that, I was never into outdoor games as I much preferred reading a good book or, better still, the latest weekly edition of "Ireland's Own."

I would spend hours reading it from cover to cover; it was full of readers' letters, jokes, and competitions, together with interesting and fascinating articles about all aspects of life in Ireland, past and present. I remember that I used to enter a lot of the competitions although I never won anything. I don't think that there was a lower age limit in the rules, but I suspect that they could tell from my large, joined up, child-like handwriting that I was probably not their ideal winner for a holiday or a car. There was usually a find-for-fun competition to locate a tiny leprechaun or pot of gold printed within the covers of the publication and I remember repeatably looking through from page to page, trying to find the small avatar. It was so much fun finding that miniature icon and I would not stop looking until I found it., so satisfying.

When I got a bit older, I started to make friends with other local children. I remember that this came about largely because of my brother, Mikey. Although he was 18 months younger than me, he found that he could mix readily with the other children in the street and so I would hang around him and gradually I became part of the crowd. As a result, I started to mix with the other children and to join in their fun and games.

Consequently, as we grew older, my brother and I would spend more and more time outside – both because we were enjoying it but also because it meant that we were not under Mothers' feet and life was a bit more relaxed. In the street where we lived, which was a quiet road with about 30 houses, most of the families had children about our age.

We used to make up our own silly games and also play street games, like "Curby" or "Gutterball" where we used to throw a leather caser football across the road and try and get a point by hitting the opposite curb or "Ackey1-2-3" a game part tag, part hide and seek, with a lamp post acting as the winning point.

During school holidays and at weekends, we used to leave our houses around 10am or after we had watched kid's programmes, such as "Tiswas" and "The Banana Splits", which was quite popular in the late 70s, early 80s. We didn't normally venture back until the streetlights came on, around 8 o'clock, normally famished but, if we were lucky, we would get a plastic beaker of squash and a crisp sandwich from one of our neighbour's moms.

Life was good while we were outside because we had all our friends to play with and we were not annoying Mom. She did not venture out of the house much, except to go to work or to do the shopping. Dad was at work, he worked long hours and so, when we went indoors, that was when things might get a little bit more stressful because there would be tension between us and with Mom, mainly with me and so we always preferred to be outdoors rather than inside.

As I got older, I used to enjoy spending more and more time with Dad. My Dad is probably the nicest man I know, and I think he helped me greatly in my life, whenever he could, and I'll always be grateful to him. When we were kids - I would have been about 10 - he would take my brother and I swimming, particularly if Mom was having one of her apocalyptic episodes. He used to treat me like an adult, even when I was just old enough to do my own school tie, and never looked down on me. My Mom would have probably told my Dad to take me out from under her feet. At his workplace, they had a sports and social club and he would take me there while he and his co-workers played snooker. They would let me play, even though I could only just get the cue over the table – remember these were full size tables. I used to really enjoy this as it made me feel more grown up but perhaps more importantly, they made me feel included and part of the grown-up gang.

On one occasion, I remember Dad saying that he had a treat lined up for me and my brother at the weekend – at that time, my youngest brother had only just been born or was still in his nappies. We couldn't wait for the next Saturday morning to come around and, to our utter amazement, Dad took us down to one of the Corporation's bus depots. While the front area was full of the latest hydraulic buses being maintained and washed, at the rear of the garage, past the inspection and re-fuel section, was the "Bus Cemetery!" Our eyes opened wide in amazement as we looked around this large open space to see row upon row of derelict and abandoned broken RouteMaster buses, just left rusting and rotting away, the majority not even in good enough condition to be used for spare parts. These buses may have been used in the late 1950's early 60's but had long since been put out of commission. You could have made a fortune on just their scrap value alone, there must have been at least fifty of them.

After this first visit, Dad would bring us down whenever we liked and we could play among the wrecks, provided we were careful and behaved ourselves. We did not need a second invitation and we were off! We had hours of fun pretending to drive the old-fashioned buses with the rear-ended open stairs with the metal poles to hold on to. Sounding the horn, moving the heavy steering wheels, and changing gear, pressing all the control buttons in the small driving cabin was such a lot of innocent fun for a couple of young boys.

We once found an old, battered and broken portable ticket machine and we pretended that we were bus conductors, going up and down the winding stairs and gangways, collecting fares. We used to find the small oblong discarded grey and brown tickets on the floor – we were fascinated at the time as we felt that we were holding a piece of history. I still remember the stale smell of cigarettes and tobacco on the bus. We had such fun. I think that Dad enjoyed taking us boys out as well. I think he also enjoyed the quiet time that this gave him being just with his boys. It was a win-win situation as Mom got her quiet time to relax by herself, while we had fun with Dad.

On a Saturday evening, we would go out as a family to one of the local dance halls. With all the Irish communities in the West Midlands, there was always somewhere to go, generally with a local band or folk group. This was a good few years after the end of the rock and roll era and I loved to watch my Mom and Dad dance and have fun. Dad was a very good dancer and I used to sit in absolute awe of him. This was the one occasion when Mom and Dad would enjoy each other's company and be relaxed together as they both loved dancing and this was their one bit of weekly entertainment.

I can remember watching him dancing with my Mom and my Aunty, one on each arm, doing the jive. They loved all the dances, including old-time-waltzes or foxtrots – it didn't matter to Dad, he could dance to any rhythm or any tune. I used to think this was amazing because I still can't dance to save my life! Meanwhile, my two brothers and I just used to sit back, watch and admire them, drinking plenty of fizzy pop and scoffing multiple packets of nearly stale crisps from the 'bargain-buy-box'. When I got older, I was the worst dancer. I couldn't imitate his style or his moves and I was forever being asked by the rest of the family "Did your Dad's dance moves skip a generation?!" I just had absolutely no dancing skills.

Chapter 2 – School Daze!

School was to form an important part of my life as I grew up – as it does for most children. However, my school days, particularly at primary school, were not happy ones. Being the son of Irish parents, I naturally went to the local Catholic primary school. I never went to nursery; due to my illness I was always in and out of hospital appointments and check-ups.

Both my brothers went to nursery, and they both went on to go to Early Years. I missed out on those experiences and I still believe that that could have had a major impact upon how I developed as a child and, perhaps, even into my teens. I truly believe that this also affected my social skills until I got much older, for I was a very quiet child who, initially, enjoyed his own company. It was not until later in my time at primary school, and with the help of my brother, who was far more outgoing, that I began to enjoy the company of other children. However, as I will explain, this was not immediately successful.

At primary school, I wasn't the smartest, but I wasn't the dumbest; I loved to read books, all types. However, I definitely wasn't the most popular. I found it difficult to make friends and I think I felt a bit embarrassed about myself - I never felt adequate, I felt ugly, I just looked at myself and thought "you just look ugly" and I used to get called names – 'Mr Piggy' or 'pig face'. I just had a bad time, I didn't mix well and ended up a bit of loner – don't get me wrong, there was nothing inadequate about my physical appearance, but I felt insecure, especially when I was name-called. I was also quite small – probably the smallest in the class, rather like the runt of the litter.

I found it hard to make new friends, unlike my brother who made friends very easily. I found that the best way for me to make friends was, instead of just hanging around the outside of a group, just to jump straight into the centre of them - not that it was funny, but it was simply a way of getting noticed. At school, I was not a boy who gathered much respect either from my classmates or from my teachers; I was just so awkward and feeble and lacked social skills. Not that I condone bullying in any way, shape, or form, I hate it with a passion but, looking back now, I must have been such an easy target.

Bullying turned out to be quite common at this school. It was not done in a blatantly obvious way but rather more subtly. For example, I would go to get my books for the next lesson, only to find that the books were missing. Eventually I would find them on a windowsill, or on a random bookcase. Wherever they were, the net result was that, time and time again, I was late into class and ended up getting detentions during mid-morning break or after school. Often, I would be shoulder charged or "bull-dozed" into the wall of the corridor or a bully would play "stamps" on my shoelaces to try to trip me up. Bullying is just the lowest and cheapest form of slapstick humour. I hated my school bullies. Some of the teachers weren't much better either and were pretty vindictive. I remember one who had a habit of frogmarching you to the headmaster's office by grabbing you by your sideburns; that was a whole lot of pain and embarrassment that my younger brother Mikey and I felt on more than one occasion!

My mother, to her credit, always made sure that we left home smartly dressed, with ironed shirts and polished shoes. We couldn't be the talk of the neighbours! I could never guarantee though that, after a school day of being pushed around and knocked about, I would return home in the same impeccable condition, but I always took the telling off with my head bowed apologetically, even then, a good reprimand from Mother was water off a duck's back.

I really wanted to be popular – you could always tell the most popular children in the class as they were usually the ones with a smile on their face; they carried a certain aura about them, and people always seemed to migrate to them. I could only watch from the periphery and feel different in some way that this was not me, but I could only hope that, one day, it would change, and I would have a great circle of friends with whom I could play.

Eventually the time came to move up to secondary school and I looked forward to it with nervous trepidation. Would my school life continue in the same way or would moving to a new environment make things different? As September came around, I became increasingly nervous and apprehensive – moving to a new school was bad enough but would the attitude of the other children be different? Would I still be picked upon? However, as I was to find out, things went wrong from the first day!

As I was the oldest son, I was the first in our family to go to secondary school and everything was new, not just for me but also for my parents, who, bless them, wanted things to be right for me. So, on the first day of the term, I set off for my new school in my new school uniform, with crisp new blazer, white shirt and smartly polished shoes.

Now, leading up to this, I had seen adults going off to work carrying their briefcase and I thought that this was the thing to do. Unfortunately, if we had looked more closely at the information sent to us from the school, we would have seen that the correct thing to use for carrying the books backwards and forwards was not a briefcase but a satchel. However, I was not aware of this and walked up to the school gate proudly carrying my briefcase with its polished gold clasp combination lock.

Now this school was the one that I had chosen; it was an all-boys school and not, by any means the worst in the city. I had chosen it because someone in my primary school had told me that this school had a table-tennis table that the boys could use. I thought, "Wow, that sounds cool, I want to go there!"

I remember on the first day I was the only one to walk into school with a briefcase and everyone just looked at me as if to say, "What are you walking into school with a briefcase for?" If I didn't have a target on my back before then that certainly had an effect! Kids were just looking at me laughing.

"Are you a teacher?"

"Hey, Sir, are you supply!?"

I replied nervously, "I just want to keep my school papers straight!"

It was downhill from then on! It's funny looking back. I mean I had never been to secondary school before and I believed that this must be part of the apparel. However, as a result, I just felt different and this made me feel uneasy around people which, in turn, made me feel extremely self-conscious. I had instantly created a great big sign above my head saying "Nerd Alert!" This was not the start that I had wished for. I wanted to merge into the school without drawing attention to myself, but my briefcase had produced just the opposite effect. I had difficulty in any case in making new friends but this episode, although planned with what we thought was the right intention, had made things even more difficult.

After a few days, I quickly realised that secondary school was what I imagined an open prison must be like - discipline was strict, rules were rigidly enforced, everyone wore identical clothes, and everyone ate their food – which was pretty bland and unappetising - in a depressing school dinner hall. I also quickly realised that there was an established hierarchy, with every new boy right at the bottom of the pile, and always at the beck and call of the senior prefects. Unfortunately, my turning up with my briefcase on day one had set me up right from the start. I was the perfect target for every bully in the school and soon began to wonder what I had done in a past life. I hated being typecast or slotted into a hole as an outsider. The thought of being on the outside petrified me and all I wanted above anything else was to be accepted. You are always safer in a group rather than excluded in isolation.

I tried my best at my school lessons, and I was rewarded by decent grades; I was conscientious enough to wake up early each weekday morning to double check that my homework was well-worded, neat and, to the best of my knowledge, correct. I always tried to give myself an extra hour before I had to get up and go to school so that I could check that I had done everything to the best of my ability and that, I think stuck with me through life – I have always stuck to the habit of double checking my work.

One of the first things to happen was that the older boys, realising that I was, in their eyes, weak and vulnerable, started demanding money in order to stop or reduce the amount of bullying – bullying that took many forms. There was a lot of name calling and ridiculing, but then it turned to physical bullying. They would come up and grab my chubby nose and shout out "Oink, Oink!" and laugh; on a few occasions, I would get a hard knuckle tap to the top of my head - all things that left no visible mark.

One of the worst things to happen, fortunately only once, was after sport, when I was in the shower and someone came up and grabbed me between the legs very painfully. I was left dazed and confused, totally unprepared as to what school life could be like. I now hated going to school, boys can be quite vicious, even at a young age. Fairly quickly I realised that, if I were to avoid getting hurt and ending up with blood on my school clothes, I would have to hand over my dinner money. I knew that if I were to go home with blood on my clothes, Mom and Dad would get both angry about the damage and anxious for my safety, which was only going to make things a whole lot worse.

The bullying continued throughout that first year, I remember one particular boy who whenever he saw me, thought it was amusing to come over and with his knuckles hit the top of my head, very hard, maybe because I was the smallest, I don't know why he did it..

"Ra-ta-tap-tap…Hello, anyone home!?" He used to shout at me.

Some mornings when I woke up, I lay in my bed trying to think up ways of avoiding going to school. However, each time, I was disabused of that idea when my Mother came up and threatened me with worse punishments if I did not get up and get ready for school.

At the school, we had a system of prefects. They were there to try and maintain order during break and lunchtime. Many of them were fair and were aware of what was happening to me but there were one or two who enjoyed adding to my misery, generally by turning a blind eye to my being bullied.

Another lesson that I learned very quickly was that labels stick. One day, a schoolboy gripped another boy's knee, in a "donkey bite" like my Dad used to give me as a kid, it was meant as a friendly gesture. But, because of this, he was labelled "gay" for the rest of his school days. He was constantly tormented, abused and bullied, all because of that one simple childish action. I felt so sorry for him, but that's the cruelty of school kids. We are all born stupid, but some kids were stupid and cruel all through their school days.

I met up with him by accident many years later in a pub in Birmingham. He was such a lovely guy; he was married with kids and totally unaffected by school life. I think he should have had a medal for what he suffered at school but, from the exterior, he was totally unblemished by the whole school experience – from the outside, it didn't look as though it had fazed him at all. However, looking back, I really felt he had had it hard.

The net result of all this bullying was that I would go home each night in a very unhappy and, frequently, sore state. Once at home, I had to hide this from Mom and Dad – although because of his shift work, he was often not home when I came home from school. Frequently, I would rush up to my room, shut the door tight and throw myself across my bed with my head under the pillow and just lay there sobbing my heart out. Was this what life at a boy's school is like, I wondered? Am I the only one who is suffering in this way? The more I thought about it, the less I could see as to a way of putting a stop to it. I had to quickly remove any signs of my sobbing before I went down for supper as otherwise, I might have faced an interrogation from Mom.

I tried to think of ways of combatting the problem but despite thinking about it for day after day, I was none the wiser.

However, after what seemed like a lifetime of misery, the summer term came to an end and I had the whole six weeks of the holiday to get over it and to spend time with my newfound friends in the street where I lived. Little did I know then that, once the new school year started, I was to find a solution to my problems. After a year of both physical and mental bullying I realised, when I had progressed a month or so into my second year of school, I had a kind of eureka moment.

I was walking to school one sunny morning, I was kicking leaves so it must have been in the autumn, I suddenly had this thought as to what I needed to do to give myself a better chance at school to stop the taunts and bullying. It dawned on me that the easiest way to stop the bullying was to try and befriend the hardest boy in the school, the toughest boy they said in all the school was Moses. I'd heard that Moses had beaten up a sixth former from another school in the school holidays for hurling abuse at his younger brother. Moses was a tall, lean mean looking boy with short black afro hair who could easily have passed for a school leaver. He exerted his influence on boys across the school by standing his ground and never running from a fight, especially with boys from other schools in our area, he was in my year but not in my class set. He was not a menace or a troublemaker, he just happened to be as hard as nails. He trained loads in all the school sports teams and was in the football team. He especially excelled in cross country running.

I was in the dinner queue, patiently waiting, when I saw him playing "slaps" with another boy. Slaps was a game where you held your hands out in a "prayer-like" position and allowed someone to slap either hand. If you moved your hand or flinched or if they missed, then it was your turn.

I asked him to give me a game, he laughed but accepted the chance to show off, I suppose. He played a game of slaps with me. Unbeknown to him, I was going to accept all the slaps and was prepared to get my hands as red-raw as necessary. He thoroughly enjoyed giving my hands a good hard slapping, he couldn't understand why my hands hardly ever flinched and from that day onwards, I became his slap partner. He thought that it was hilariously funny that I never flinched or moved my hands. Little did he know! If anyone else asked me for a game of slaps, I'd politely decline.

This umbilical cord connection to Moses carried some weight with other school kids. From that moment on, if ever I was in a situation where I was alone and I was going to have my dinner money taken or felt unsafe, I would shout out his name and ask if anyone had seen him as he wanted to talk with me.

"Anyone seen Moses?" I'd shout.

This normally caused a bit of confusion and bought me some time to run off to try to find him, even though I was never looking for him in the first place. I would just shout his name.

Another way in which I avoided problems was through my love of reading. At any given opportunity, I would dash off to the school library, partly to get away from everyone who could cause me problems. I was no book worm, but I did try my best at school, and I enjoyed reading. I always wanted to please my parents, especially my Dad, with whom I had a special connection. It was not so much a library, as that was probably too grand a word for just a dusty windowless room with a dozen or so shelves of books, mostly tattered copies of journals, gifted books by parents or old returns, much as you might expect to find in an open prison! However, it had a few chairs and a couple of tables, I would find solace there and would fill every moment reading about different parts of the world, of scientific discoveries, of the possibility of space travel, now that man had landed on the moon, and many other exciting subjects. Here I could fly under the radar and lose myself for forty minutes or so in a different world, alone but happy and secure.

I soon found out that to survive school, I had two main assets in my locker – my resistance to pain during hand slapping and the ability to make other kids laugh! I was never going to outfight them – after all, I was a tiny, podgy little kid. I would however make up funny, ridiculous songs that I would sing, partly to get me noticed and partly to create a crowd so I was no longer a target, you can't bully someone in the middle of a crowd.

I was no Ed Sheeran, but I tried to make up silly tunes. I remember making up a song about having a Rubik's Cube and blasted out few lines of rubbish at school break time. This made everyone laugh at me which, in turn, raised my status from a nobody to a small-time somebody who could make people laugh. For the first time, they could see a positive side to me and that benefitted me – it was my inbuilt safety mechanism kicking in! I got out of being punched or kicked – I just made them laugh.

There were many things that happened while I was at that school, some good and some bad but there is one story that I will never forget. To this day, I do not know whether or not this story that I am going to tell you is true but what I do know is that all of us who heard it never ever forgot it!

Apparently, or so the story goes, one of the boys was out in the playground when a pregnant fly flew into his eye and got behind the eye. It then proceeded to lay its eggs, which hatched in the warm comfortable surroundings and the maggots, while looking for food, found the back of the eye much to their liking and proceeded to eat it. As I said, I do not know if this is, or even could be, true but, I think that you can imagine the impression that it made on 11-year old boys!

Not all my school days were bad days, however. In my fifth and final year at that school, I was called to the PE teacher's study. I was proper scared because normally, this type of summons was the prelude to a slapping with the gym shoe (pump) across the backside or, worse still, the belt buckle.

The PE teacher, who we used to nickname Paddy because he was Irish, reminded me of the comedian from Cannon and Ball. He was the school's oldest and only salaried bully and dished out the pump and belt on a regular basis. His skills at whipping off his belt and proceeding to give out lashes, sent fear around the school and were legendary.

Normally being called into Paddy's office meant getting red painful welts around the back of your legs. However, I was in for a very different shock. When I got to his office, I found myself, along with nine other boys, all queuing up to enter his office. We were called in turn and I was amazed to discover that we were not being called to be punished – just the opposite as we were all being made prefects for the last part of our school life! To this day, I do not know what I had done to deserve this honour – for an honour it most definitely was – but I suppose that the staff must have thought that I had done something right otherwise they would not have picked me. Prefects get the cushiest jobs and all the perks, so I was just so chuffed to get the badge. Not going to lie - it was probably my happiest moment. How sad was that!

I left school that year with five "O" level passes, not brilliant grades but all passes. I was just happy to get out alive and still have my body and face in working order. I reflected on school life and what I had learned. It taught me most of all a decent life lesson, make the right acquaintances.

Of course, there was the basic level of a solid, if not outstanding, education but what was there that was more than that – what did I bring from it into the wider world? If I am honest, I must confess that the aim of the school system is to prepare you for the big wide world and hopefully to set you up with the possibility of getting a job. For some of my classmates, it was no secret but that a hard life ahead beckoned, either in one of the local factories or slogging away in the heat of one of the many steelworks spread throughout Birmingham and the Black Country. My Dad worked as a bus driver in the city and although he worked long hours and often shifts across the day, he did not have to suffer hard manual labour day in and day out. I don't think that the same was going to happen to many of my classmates. There were not many office-based white-collar jobs around in our area and so the thought of going on to further education seemed like a good call.

So, what did I learn? With hindsight, secondary school is a learning experience to give you basic skills to progress. I would not have changed anything about it. I never made any lifelong friends there, but I still learned some decent growing up skills – I think that it gave me a certain degree of maturity. It was a series of stepping-stones where you learn about life – hopefully it teaches you not to fall into the same traps twice! I never got into trouble at school as I was too scared of my Mom, but I never mixed well, and I always found it difficult to make friends. I was not popular, and I suppose that if you asked any of the kids who attended that school when I was there, for those five years between 1981 and 1986, most would not be able to put a face to the name.

I just felt different and this made me feel uneasy around people which, in turn, probably gave off a bad vibe or negative aura. I think some of my problems stemmed from the few years I had as a result of the operation that I underwent for a pelvic disease, which meant that I was not able to socialise with other children at a key stage in my life when other children were building friendships. I lacked social conformity, but I didn't miss it, I just didn't know I needed it. As the oldest sibling, you make all the first mistakes, so others learn from you.

I learned a lot in terms of a basic education but, from a personality point of view, my key lessons learned were the ability to make people laugh, both at me and with me; I learned how to fly under the radar, thereby escaping trouble and serious problems both from school mates and from teachers. I also learned how to make friends with the right people. These lessons worked for me, although they might not have worked for other boys, but they did save me from a lot of beatings. As I walked out of school on that last day, I felt that I must have done something right during my time at school, I had been made a school prefect. I must have impressed someone. Did I do the usual thing and write my name on everyone's shirt, get emotional and hug everyone like most people did? Did I heck! Truth be told I walked quickly out of the front gates and didn't look back.

Open-Prison, I mean Secondary School, was now behind me, a chapter of my life from which I would move on. As I picked up speed, I began to jog back home and slowed after running as far as possible. I remember wondering what the hell to do next, where was my path taking me and whether any of these life lessons were going to work for me now that I was out in the big wide and cruel world, or was I at the start of a completely new learning curve, facing a whole lot of new problems? I didn't know what the morrow would bring but I was scared and nervous about what my future would hold. I had completed the compulsory school system, got out alive and had got the shirt and prefect-badge to prove it.

In later years I used to wonder what happened to Moses, who unwittingly helped me more than he ever realised. I did do a few checks online and social media, but his name never returned any hits. I would love to thank him one day as this one boy was my school saviour, so if you do ever read this book, Moses – "Thank you for being the best slaps partner anyone could have asked for!"

Chapter 3 – My Happy Place

Although I was born and raised in the West Midlands, both my parents were from good Catholic stock from Ireland, my father from the West and my mother from Northern Ireland. Dad had moved to Birmingham to get employment in the early 1960s and had met and married Mom over here, to where all her family had already migrated. However, Dad's family still lived on the west coast where they continued to run a small farm in County Galway. All of Ireland is a beautiful place, a real treasure and I would say to anyone who hasn't been to go and experience it yourself.

Because Mom and Dad had jobs that were not particularly the best paid, we, like many others of our generation, used to have just one week's holiday a year, topped up, when possible with special days out to places like Blackpool and Weston-Super-Mare. During the six weeks holiday, the cost of holidays doubles, as it's a busy time with the kids being off school, so we had to save all year to pay for this one holiday. But it was traditional, we went every year and so, as a family, it was a very special holiday to look forward to, a big wave goodbye to England and a warm hello to Ireland. People smile when they are happy and everyone in Ireland smiles. That was always how I felt about the Irish people, probably the friendliest in the world. I've now travelled a lot, but I have never found a happier and warmer group of people. If you lived over there and saw the beauty of the country and breathed in the nature and the traditional Irish way of life, it is totally intoxicating and draws you in straight away. Definitely put it on your bucket list, I guarantee you will thank me.

Because Dad's family still had their farm, it meant that all he had to pay for was the cost of the ferry and car fuel for, once we got to Co Mayo, we lived with Dad's family in a small rural town just outside Roscommon. Nevertheless, it was still hard for Mom and Dad to save the money for the holiday. The cost of living was, and probably still is, quite high over there and, in those days, 'Chip and Pin' was not invented. So, Dad invariably had to bring enough cash to cover our stay hence, probably, why we only ever went for a week at a time. In fact, Dad often use to work overtime to make some extra money towards our holiday. However, on the plus side, it was a week that the whole family, both in Birmingham and in Co Mayo, looked forward to and so, I suppose, that mitigated the difficulties in saving the money.

Dad initially had an old Ford Cortina and then, later, a more modern if less stylish Maxi – boy, did he love that car! It was his pride and joy. We would pack the car to within an inch of its life, to the point where we were sitting on our own suitcases. In those days, it was not compulsory to wear seat belts, so we never bothered. We probably wouldn't have been able to anyway with all the luggage.

We always set off very early in the morning for the journey, mostly to avoid the traffic but also to try and steer clear of the police, as we were probably over our car's carrying capacity and must have been in breach of the law or some health and safety regulation. We drove for about four hours up through North Wales and then along the North Wales coast and over the bridge into Anglesey and on to Holyhead where our car-ferry would be waiting for us to drive on board. We enjoyed driving on to the boat, it added to our whole holiday experience.

We all loved this holiday, not just because we were getting away for a week but, firstly it gave Dad a chance to see all his extended family and secondly, for us boys, it was a chance to spend a week in a magical wonderland, a different lifestyle and culture, so different from our home life in Birmingham. Furthermore, Mom and Dad were able to relax with the wider family and there were none of the arguments and discord that were such a feature of our normal home life. For us, it was the best week of the year and probably, upon reflection, better than birthday and Christmas combined!

Once on the boat, we could go and explore. It was fun on the ferry, we would stand on the deck as the ferry pulled slowly out of Holyhead harbour, waving to the people on the dockside and to those on the smaller boats as we went passed, chuckling as we saw these little toy boats being rocked from side to side and up and down from the bow wave as our ferry steamed majestically by, giving the occasional hoot if the crew thought that other boats were getting too close. Mom always made sandwiches and squash that we were able to sit and enjoy on board ship as we sailed across the Irish Sea towards Dublin, a couple of hours by boat and we were in another country!

Once we got to Ireland, the journey was far from over as we had approximately 200-250km to drive across some very variable country roads, roads that got a little better and wider as we journeyed towards the coast in Co Mayo. The journey was through a variety of landscapes. Co Mayo is the third largest in area of Southern Ireland's 21 counties and is bounded to the west by the Atlantic Ocean – sometimes, we boys would stand on the cliff and look out to sea, wondering what was on the other side. There is a definite difference between the west of the county and the east – the west coast area of Co Mayo, where my grandparents lived, has poor soil quality and has large areas of blanket bog or peatland, and is not much good for farming whereas the east side of the county, is largely limestone and offers much better farming conditions.

Eventually, after about two-and-three-quarter hours we would see the farm up ahead and we boys would cheer and start to bounce up and down in the car as we could feel the excitement mounting. Mom would turn around and shout at us to calm down but, for once, it was said with a smile as she knew just how much this all meant to Dad and to us. As we drove up to the small farmhouse bungalow, there were Grandad and Grandma always standing on the doorstep, arms wide open, big smiles on their faces, waiting to give us enormous welcoming hugs. As we got to the doorway, we could smell the most delicious smells coming from the kitchen – Grandma was a wonderful cook, unlike Mom, and we could smell something cooking and, in the background there was the even more wonderful smell of her homemade cakes, which, if we were lucky, we might get one each as a treat before our evening meal. The kitchen was the heart of and soul of the farm – it was also the warmest place with its big AGA stove that was always kept alight, burning peat logs. What a start to the holiday! Goodbye Birmingham, hello Heaven!

All too soon, after a wonderful supper of meat and fresh vegetables that Grandad had grown in his garden, followed by a big bowl of home-made ice cream and fresh fruit - late strawberries, gooseberries and plums – it was time for bed. Being an old farmhouse right out in the country, it did not have central heating and so we boys all shared one bed –

we never minded but, if we had been asked to share a bed at home, then we would have kicked off. Here, we were on holiday in a different world. The farm didn't have any of the modern things like an inside toilet – that was outside and so you made sure that you went before you went to bed as it was not a lot of fun, poking about in the dark to get there and back, there were always eerie sounds that made you jump. Just as you were venturing down the paved path, something would normally suddenly fly or run across your path which would of course make you need to run to the toilet even quicker. Nature and nature-calling working in perfect harmony!

In the morning, we were up, washed in a large beautifully painted free-standing ceramic wash basin, then dressed and ready for breakfast. This venture into a more basic type of existence might sound like we were in some kind of boot camp but to us kids it was all a really exciting adventure and we relished the way other people lived and went about their normal household duties. I remember it was all just fun.

The home cooked smells of freshly-made breakfast was a delight and initiated instant 'feed me' rumblings in the stomach, hardly anything needed to be shop bought. A cooked breakfast was a great way to set us up for the day. Nothing like the cereal or toast we had back home, normally we might have some liver, bacon and fried onions for breakfast with homemade soda bread and washed down with cups of tea. I remember the food was always served on old, large, blue and white plates with farmyard scenes painted on them. Portion sizes were always large and generous. Gran thought it was strange not to eat everything on the plate and if you picked at your food slowly, she would smile and call you a little bird.

I remember my Grandad was a quiet man of few words and he would sit down at the head of the kitchen table and holding his knife and fork in each hand would tilt his head, close his eyes and say a few words of grace and then commence eating without murmuring another word, head down parallel to his plate with wooden handled knife and fork carving his food in perfect harmony, I was always amused by how he didn't seem to look up from his plate while he ate, only on occasion pausing to digest his food and to take a gulp of fresh morning milk from his glass. I would sit mesmerised by him, just watching him carve, chew, swallow and repeat, never pausing or stopping.

Bearing in mind that he had probably been up a few hours already, as soon as he had finished his breakfast, he would get up and wander over to his large comfy single chair next to the oven and get out his pipe and bag of tobacco, light it with a match and gently with a few good sucks get the tobacco burning red and the pipe smoke began filling the kitchen, I just loved the smell of pipe smoke and it always brings back such happy memories. The used matchstick was then disposed into the AGA oven, no waste. He sat back, relaxed, and quietly read his morning paper from start to finish, every single word, article, and story. He enjoyed reading while listening to the radio. I loved to watch him reading and puffing away on his wooden pipe, I was totally transfixed.

The one thing I could never get used to was the ultra-fresh milk. I never drank it on its own as it hadn't been pasteurised. It was probably the tastiest milk you could imagine but I wasn't too keen. It just wasn't what I was used to.

Once breakfast was over, there were not the usual chores such as we had to do at home but, instead, Grandad and

Grandma had different ones for us – ones that we enjoyed doing, probably because they were different. There was milk to be brought into the kitchen from the milk churns, turf to get from the large open shed and stored by the AGA in the kitchen and, probably most fun of all, chasing the chickens while we were supposed to be collecting the eggs!

Unlike at home, we never minded these chores for we were helping and were being treated like grown-ups rather than as children. We all loved it on the farm, for what it lacked in resources, it more than compensated for in terms of wide-open spaces and loads of areas in which to play and hide. We made up all sorts of games, pretending to be soldiers in the war or robbers in the woods. You name it, we made it up and played it. We normally went straight out after breakfast and didn't go back in until it was time to wash up for dinner.

Bearing in mind it was summertime, the weather was always warm as we got the gentle breeze from the Atlantic sea. I remember helping out on the farm with my Dad, my brother Mikey and Grandad, building giant haystacks and jumping on them for hours whilst the hay was being manually tossed up on top of the haystack and us kids compounding it down by jumping on it, no modern day combine harvesters doing the work, all manual labour. Then, later, we went off by tractor to the turf bog, a big area of moorland owned by my Grandad - he had an acre or so of peat land and we would watch my Dad and Grandad dig hundreds of turf bricks to store in the turf shed.

There was always a job to be done and never an idle moment. It really is a hard job being a farmer, all manual labour in those days but it is totally rewarding and satisfying work. It keeps you extremely fit and healthy. We did literally work all day until the cows came home! My

Dad always enjoyed helping on the farm as these were jobs that he had done from an early age with his brother, there was always good banter and laughs as they worked hard, drank tea from flasks and ate sandwiches from inside a linen napkin. And, best still, when we had a quiet moment between jumping on haystacks, we got to ride the donkey (called Captain) up and down the back field, picking gooseberries from the shrub as we sat on his back. They were lovely, cherished memories and ones that will stay with me forever.

A favourite part of our Irish holidays, especially if our other cousins came over to the farm for a visit, was going out in the evenings to the local quaint pub in the village where we were staying. Because of the number of occasions that we had visited these pubs, they always welcomed us and remembered us from our previous visits, and especially Dad from when he was a young man growing up in the town. There would be a roaring fire and usually a sing song with either a few of the regulars on the flute and fiddle, or it might be a proper three-piece band with vocals, banjo, and keyboard. They were fantastic evenings and on more than one occasion Dad would jive with one of the local women and give her a twirl around the small space in the bar. Our cousins would always be great fun and company, I really miss those evenings when even Mom and Dad seemed to be so relaxed and happy in each other's company, I think it's the Irish hospitality, or it might be the Guinness! People in Ireland are genuinely laid back, relaxed and friendly – I honestly believe that they are one of the friendliest nations on the planet.

We didn't spend all week at the farm for Dad had relatives all over the place and so this was our opportunity to meet up with our extended family – aunts, uncles and cousins – and I think that they used to enjoy our visits as much as we enjoyed being with them. They were a novelty to us, with their soft rural Irish brogue and we were certainly unusual to them, being townies with a completely different attitude to everything and our 'Brummie' accent. Another aspect of visiting our cousins was that they all lived in such beautiful homes, homes that were far bigger and grander than anything we could ever have dreamed of living in, let alone owning. Normally these homes were by the sea and, as most homes over there were built individually, you tended to build your own home to your own bespoke specification, design and budget– to us they were like grand mansions.

We loved visiting a couple of cousins we had in Galway, they were of similar ages to myself and Mike and we always had fun. They were so mischievous and loved having a laugh. I remember on one occasion we went to a nearby amusement arcade – what an adventure for a "towny" like me! – where we got into trouble for "flicking." We found a long small, thin, bendy branch and stripped off all the leaves and side shoots, creating a long, flexible bendy-wand which we used to insert into the lower pay-out section of the slot machine. This was one of those arcade games like you see today on 'Tipping Point' on TV, where, as the coins drop and push others over the edge, a large number remain, hanging over the edge, waiting to be pushed and we would snake the stick back up until it reached the lowest level where the coins were on the verge of falling I would use our stick to flick the edges of the coins and cause them all to drop down while my cousin would block the view as I knocked off loads of 10p pieces. We regularly collected several quid which we used to buy fish and chips but, on one occasion, we were spotted by the employees and had to leg it fast before they caught us! We were too young to consider the consequences – to us it was just a game, a way of making some money and of having a laugh. We were only about 12 years old at the time.

One of our cousins lived in a large house near the beach, in a town outside Dublin. It had a long drive with beautiful landscaped gardens. They were obviously well off, as I asked once what my uncle did for a living and my dad said that he had sold his business, retired early and now enjoyed a game of golf. I just remember thinking that sounded like such a fantastic thing to be able to do. We thought this was the biggest house we'd ever slept in, like a 4-star hotel and we just loved going there, especially as there were four cousins of a similar age to us.

Our only regret was the short amount of time that we could spend there. We used to jump out of the car, meet up with our cousins and run straight down to the beach, where it was shirts, shorts, shoes and socks off and straight into the sea for a quick swim before the grown-ups could stop us. On a warm summer's day, this was sheer ecstasy. It was then back up to the house, towel off under the steely eye of Mom, get dressed and sit down to tea. If Dad had planned it correctly, we would stay overnight there and we would be playing and laughing in our rooms with our cousins until it was time for bed, trying hard not to be heard by the parents. After all the adults had gone to bed, that's when we got back up, as planned and went over to a quieter part of the house for more fun, games and midnight snacks. I am sure that they did hear us and knew exactly what was going on, but Aunt and Uncle stopped Mom and Dad from ruining our fun. My Aunty and Uncle were such lovely, adorable, and sincere people and would do anything for anyone. Really genuine and I loved them dearly.

We had the very best of times there and it was always the highlight at the end of our family holiday, although all of it was great. I learned the basic skills of playing a real piano while we were there, being taught by my cousin, I still remember to this day how to play "Annie's Song" by John Denver. I always used to think that they were extremely rich for, not only did they have this massive house and gardens with all the latest fashions and luxuries but I remember on one occasion when we visited, they showed us the very latest CD player. I thought that this was awesome when compared to our old record player back in Birmingham.

Our annual holiday to Ireland was probably the time that Mom and Dad were at their happiest, both together and with the family. All the stresses and strains of everyday life at home had been forgotten and we simply enjoyed each moment for exactly what it was – a fantastic, once-a-year holiday with the extended family. My brothers and I always left Ireland with more money in our pockets than when we first arrived from all our relatives! It was only when we got off the ferry at Holyhead and started the drive back home, that the problems and quarrels started all over again.

I personally never liked leaving Ireland, it was so heart-wrenching to leave those places and people that I loved so much and to return to a place so different. It's strange and sad, having said all that, I have never, to this day, been back to Ireland, it's been over twenty-five years to date. I would genuinely love to go back to the peace and tranquillity of that warm and welcoming country. I miss the places that we used to visit in Ireland, Mayo, Dublin, Galway and all the other wonderful towns in between that are still so fresh in my mind, almost as if it were yesterday. I know that places and people are always changing, families sell up and emigrate and many people say you should never go back as it will not be the same. That might be why I've never returned, afraid of bursting the dream bubble. Deep down, I'd be sad to think that the Ireland I loved as a child, that I loved so dearly, is any different now. "No, nay never no more!"

Chapter 4 – The Black Sheep

I always felt that if Carlsberg ever made 'Black Sheep' then I would win the title of 'Black Sheep of The Family' – I never quite fitted in at school or at home. I always felt self-conscious about my looks and my appearance, my body, my personality – I always felt different in some way. I knew something wasn't quite right, when after turning 16, my auntie, who worked in banking and is such a lovely dear lady, she was my Mom's sister, bought me a beautiful presentation case full of all the coins from the year I was born, dated 1969. It was lovely present, and all the uncirculated pristine coins had been displayed carefully inside a well-crafted velvet case, with a certificate of authenticity. It should have been something to cherish for years and was more of an investment item as she was from banking. Within half an hour of her wishing me a happy birthday and leaving, the display box had been roughly dismantled and broken open, all the coins had been pocketed to buy some scallop and chips from the local Chippy, chips in the bag are the best! I used to tear a hole in the top right corner and love eating the chips from inside the paper bag, plenty of salt and vinegar and let the steam escape from the bag...Delicious!

I love my food. I loved to eat anything, well almost anything, apart from the food that Mom brought home from work. As I explained earlier, Mom worked as a cashier in the catering department of the local geriatric hospital in Moseley, close to where we lived. At the end of her shift, when the cafeteria was closing, the staff could take home, free of charge, any of the left-over food from that day. Mom was a frugal person who saw this as a way of saving money, while not letting good food go to waste!

The result was that we hated evening meals from Monday to Thursday. We knew as soon as we saw her walking up our road to our house carrying some bags, that we were in for yet another "culinary nightmare." Normally, inside the large plastic bags were silver-foiled green ceramic bowls filled with the cold leftover hospital meals, with great dollops of cold greasy gravy liberally applied on top, all looking totally unedifying but just waiting to be reheated. The pudding was no better, as the desert had cold, congealed custard, complete with skin, liberally applied for good measure. To this day, I can't abide thick skin on any food product, be it meat or pudding!

I am not being a food prude about our mother's freebies, but it really did not look appetising and tasted even worse! It was then micro-waved, and the countdown timer commenced. Mom told us umpteen times that she didn't have to pay for these "delightful" dishes as, otherwise, they would have ended up being binned, so she considered it employees' perks – free dinner and desert. She came from a background where you use what you have and never let anything go to waste. I know we didn't have a lot of money and I know that this was a cost-efficient way of saving money, but my brothers and I all hated this hospital food, and, even to this day, I doubt I would be able to eat it.

When my Mom popped the bowls into the microwave to reheat the food, I knew a battle of minds was about to commence. She would say to me "You get to eat good wholesome food"

"But, Mom, nobody wanted it, that's why it's leftover food, it tastes and looks horrible. Look at the thick skin on the gravy and custard"

To which she retorted "You'd be glad to eat it if you lived in Africa!"

I replied "Well, post it to Africa and see if they enjoy it!"

"You are such an ungrateful little boy"

"It's going to make me sick, Mom, it's leftover food and it looks and tastes disgusting"

"You will eat it, if I tell you to!"

"No, I will not Mom, it's going to make me throw up!"

"Well go to bed hungry then!"

"I will!"

"Wait till I tell your father when he gets home"

Whereupon, I might have become a little sarcastic and said, "Don't forget to save him some!" I would just try whatever it took to get up to my room in one piece without her getting the belt on me. She never came up to my room to make sure that I was OK, or even to offer me something different – I'd made my choice and so, as far as she was concerned, I was stuck with it. But that was my Mother!

You would have thought that, with these battles, day after day, she would have given up the fight to get us to eat the food, but she never stopped trying – she just kept bringing it home. However, in total contrast to that, we absolutely loved Fridays. On Friday, our luck changed - we always had Saveloy, chips and curry sauce. We could not afford a large fish for each of us, but we were quite happy with Saveloys from the local chippy which we loved, complete with extra batter bits. Oh, how we looked forward to Fridays – a few chips, dipped in curry sauce was a heavenly treat compared to the previous nights' dishes. Fridays could not come around quick enough So that was our one treat of the week. On Saturdays we tended to snack on whatever was in the larder or bread bin, whereas, on Sundays, we had a sit-down Sunday dinner, when Mom and Dad made sure that we all sat down as a family round the table together.

When I was about 16 or 17, there was an incident that was to have a massive impact upon our family. I went into the kitchen looking for something, can't remember what, and started rummaging about in the lower cupboards. There was this sweet, syrupy pungent smell that I first noticed, the smell hit the back of my throat and nostrils. To my bewilderment, at the back of the cupboard was a large plastic bag, the bag had been inadvertently left untied, by mistake I presume. In it I found a whole collection of miniature whisky, rum, and vodka bottles. Young as I was, I realised that this was not normal, but I did not know what to do for the best. I was worried and scared so I went and found my Dad. Looking back, I think that he was already aware that Mother had become an alcoholic but even he was shocked at the sheer volume of miniature bottles that had been hidden. I have often wondered since why she had hung on to them and not thrown them away – perhaps she was afraid the neighbours might see her putting them in the dustbin or maybe she was hoping that we would find them as a plea for help. Who knows?

Strangely, finding all this evidence of alcohol made me feel guilty – not because I had informed on her to Dad but because I felt, deep down, that I might be the root cause of her turning to the bottle. I began to feel that, maybe, if I had been a better child and son to her then, perhaps, she might not have found it necessary to turn to alcohol as the solution. Mother never admitted that she was an alcoholic and that she was also addicted to pills, but I understand that one of the typical symptoms of being an addict – be it alcohol, drugs or both - is that you still think that you are in complete control of what you are doing. However, she was definitely on a Hell ride to oblivion. She needed help but her help was out of my control, maybe after telling Dad, he would do something, I didn't know what, but I knew he got on well with my Nan, so maybe he might confide in my Mom's Mom.

As young boys growing up, we enjoyed visiting was our Nan's home – my Mom's mother. Nan and my Grandad lived in an old terraced house in Alum Rock, near the centre of Birmingham. The house was always busy, with a constant ebb and flow of people coming in and out, family members popping in on their way to and from work for tea and biscuits. There were a lot of brothers and sisters in my Nan's family, a typically big Irish family, who all lived within spitting distance of each other, making a significant contribution to the Irish community in the area. We had some very happy times there as we grew up.

You'd come in, sit yourself down and Nan would emerge from the kitchen, normally with a cup of tea in her hand – she knew straight away that there would be someone wanting a cup of tea. Then more would come in for breakfast, with another wave coming for sandwiches at lunchtime. My Nan was a conveyor belt of hot and cold food. She was constantly preparing meals in the kitchen – that's basically where she lived. All the best china and furniture was in the front room, which was always kept spick and span, and only used on special occasions, as was common in many houses in the city in those days.

My Nan was a little bit of an eccentric, she is the only person I know who used to kiss spiders she found in the bath. Nan called them money spiders and used to think they would bring her good luck! She would also cross her two forefingers whenever she saw a solitary magpie and if she ever saw the politician Ian Paisley on the TV then a word of advice - put in some earplugs as she would turn the air blue! She spent most of her day in a small narrow kitchen at the back of the house, unless of course the horse racing was on and her favourite jockey, Pat Eddery, was racing. She loved the racing. She never drank and she never smoked but she did have a little flutter every now and then on the horses, maybe a 10p each way accumulator on some of Eddery's rides. So, whenever Pat Eddery was racing, normally on a Saturday afternoon, Grandad and Nan would sit down in front of the TV with a cup of tea, a slice of fruit cake each and both would enjoy watching and cheering on their favourite jockey.

I was always astounded by the amount of footfall and the number of people coming in and out of that one building. Looking back, I'm surprised. At best it could have passed for a busy café and at worst, well the police might have suspected criminal activity and have had it under surveillance! It was such a busy hub of activity.

My Nan was a great cook; she had a wealth of cookery skills and could make all sorts of bread and cakes, Irish bread, soda bread, fruit bread – you name it and she could throw her hand at it.

I'm biased but she was a lovely adoring Nan and is sadly missed. I loved it most when she would let me dip my warm freshly made soda bread into the beef roasting tin, when she was cooking the Sunday beef – that soggy, dipped bread with its meaty flavour and goodness, it was "Manna from Nanna!" It was the very best! In years to come, I used to think about that soggy, dipped beef bread and this was one of my nicest memories when I was starving and at my lowest ebb. I often used to think back on those happy days with Nan and Grandad. They were some of my fondest memories with Nan shouting at the TV for Pat to "hit the whip" over the last furlong, I loved them both dearly.

However, typically, my home life could not have been more different than being at my grandparents' and it was here that Mom and me were normally at loggerheads. I used to have some almighty arguments with my Mom. I remember one such occasion vividly, when I was still living at home and having the mother of all arguments with her. I had been out one night and met a girl whom I had known at primary school and I had promised to call her when I got home to make sure that she had got home safe and sound.

When I got home it was quite late and everyone was in bed. I looked at the phone - it was one of the old-style dial-up phones and Mom had fitted a metal lock on the cradle so that we boys could not use it and run up large bills. However, I knew how to bypass the phone lock by tapping the numbers on the black cradle (for all you born after 1985 you might need to Google the old-style dial up phone up on the internet!).

Anyway, all my tapping must have woken my mother by the loud rat-tap-tapping on the phone cradle and she came storming downstairs to investigate. She was in a foul mood, as I had woken her up, she was a very light sleeper and she started screaming hells-bells at me. I think, at that moment, that I just saw all the colours, especially red and all the years of absorbing the abuse from her finally came to a head and a massive altercation ensued, whereupon I ended up running at pace towards her, grabbing her with both fists around the lapels of her night gown and pushing her hard and forcefully away from me against the door frame She was in utter shock. In her eyes I saw a combination of fear, doubt, shock, and a major dose of disappointment as you might imagine, and I was mortified that I had pushed my mother so forcefully. She panicked and ran back upstairs. Fortunately for me, I think my Dad was on late shift that night.

As I went to bed, I thought that, once daylight comes, I had best leave and pack my bags. I was in a desperate predicament and, above all, I was afraid that, when Dad found out what had happened, he would be bitterly disappointed and heartbroken with me. Everything had got on top of me and all the angst and pain over the years which had built up inside had reached a pinnacle.

In the morning, I walked out of the house, before everyone else was awake, I only had one thought and that was I couldn't survive another day, I wanted to kill myself, I honestly believed this was the last day of my life, I was in a desperate state mentally. I couldn't take it anymore and my brain was in turmoil. I couldn't see my next move and all my options seemed to have Mother in a better position – Queen – Checkmate! She held all the cards. She set all the rules in the house, what she said went and she was a strict disciplinarian. We had a massive conflict of interest.

I hated the idea of going home and I remember to this day travelling all day on the same bus, round the same route on the number 11 bus in Birmingham, which travels in a large 25-mile circle. I was just going bat-shit crazy with the idea of going home, hated the idea of another run in with my Mom. I was 17, coming 18 and felt like an adult but, at the same time, I felt that I was being treated like a child. I had only loose change and no idea what I was supposed to do.

After about eight hours of just riding on various number 11 buses, I found that I only had a total of about £3.50 in loose change in my pocket. I got off the bus, went to a late night pharmacy and bought a large bottle of 50 Paracetamol – the strongest ones that they would sell me over the counter – I went back home as late as possible, once I thought that it was late enough for them to be in bed – around about 10/10.30 pm. Everything was switched off, the house was in darkness, everyone was in bed. I know now this was an act of desperation, maybe to deflect Dad's anger at me for grabbing and pushing my Mother the night before. I contemplated swallowing the full bottle; this surely out trumps any physical assault on my Mother, doesn't it? That's how my mind was working and how screwed up mentally I was. I probably should have been institutionalised!

I remember going to the bathroom and taking all the tablets in one go with a large glass of cold water. I then just sat on the floor and waited for the tablets to kick in and for death to take me. I know that this must sound like the coward's way out, but I had already gone over the brink, having consumed those 50 tablets and I was just lying on the bathroom floor, locked in. I just presumed that I was going to die there because I didn't expect anyone to come into the bathroom, not that late at night anyway. I just felt young, naïve and unworthy of life but as fate would have it, I was just succumbing to the effect of the tablets when my Dad either decided that he needed to go to the toilet or maybe he had a sixth sense that something was not right, or he had not been asleep and heard me coming back.

I will always remember that night. There was me, lying on the bathroom floor waiting to die and there was Dad knocking loudly on the door, "Sean, are you in there?" But, obviously, he wasn't getting any response. I think that Dad suspected that something was wrong, the toilet door being locked. After about five minutes without any response, he broke the door off its hinges to find me lapsing into unconsciousness and shouted for help, telling my Mom to call the ambulance.

I think my attempt at suicide was in some way an attempt to deflect from the pain, the humiliation and embarrassment of the night before, when I had the major altercation with my Mother. I was lost and honestly felt without hope. I don't remember being taken away at speed to hospital, but I do remember lying on the hospital table, lights above me, doctors all around me, sticking a long tube down my throat into my stomach to pump out all the toxins and tablets. That feeling of heaving up all the bile and sick over the edge of the table into a bowl will remain with me for ever.

Mentally I was in a very, very bad way. I just did not know where I was going with my life, I could see no future. My Mother and me – it was just a terrible situation to be in, not just for her but also for the rest of the family and the only answer I could think of was to take myself out of the equation completely and therefore to be gone. However, the medics and staff saved me but what was the future going to hold? I was a total wreck, in absolute misery, maybe with hindsight I should have died that night?

Chapter 5 – Dreams Squashed!

I was still feeling the strains and trauma of having my stomach pumped out and was feeling totally embarrassed by the situation. It definitely wasn't a family topic of discussion and was quickly swept under the carpet. I don't think any of the rest of the family were aware that I had tried to commit suicide. It became a taboo subject. I was offered no comfort by anyone and just had to store my feelings up inside.

In those days, there was no after-event help, care or counselling offered. I left hospital and was just suffering mentally. I must have been so depressed, but I still had my life to live, I was young, and I quickly realised I was so grateful to be alive. I know that I remembered thanking God for giving me a second chance. I had to try and decide what I was going to do with it. So, after about a week of recuperation, although it felt like only a couple of days, I had to make a very quick decision of either going on to further education which was my preference or getting a job, which was what my Mom wanted me to do.

While both myself and my middle brother, Mike tried to do our best at school, neither of us were particularly the cleverest in our class, unlike my youngest brother who had everything – brains, talent, and dedication. However, one of the lessons that I really enjoyed at secondary school was chemistry, a selection that was encouraged by my Auntie who was a head nun at a school; she is passionate about the subject and has a PhD in chemistry. It was for these reasons that I decided that I wanted to go to sixth form college to study chemistry when I left school. I know it was against my Mom's wishes, but I wanted to try and get my A-Levels and go for a well-paid job at the end of my education.

Birmingham, being a big industrial city, has a plethora of technical colleges and I found one that I liked the look of and was offering the type of course that I wanted. I signed on and when the term started in September, I settled down to a life of study that I knew was going to be hard but exhilarating when compared to school. It was a class of 30 student, almost all male with a couple of females of our own age. They came from a variety of backgrounds and some were more interested in learning than others – no different to school really! This was going to be a walk in the park.

I had decided to take maths, chemistry and physics as my A-Level exams. I had enjoyed them at school and thought I would do well with them in college. Sitting in the class on the first day, I really did not know what to expect. Looking round, I could see that some were looking slightly apprehensive, while others were playing the "big boy, look at me" approach. The next thing I knew the lecturer was striding in, purposefully. He was a tall man of about 55, glasses and going slightly bald. He introduced himself and then started to outline the course and what would happen. He explained that there were three lecturers on the course, and each would take a different part of the syllabus.

Our chemistry lecturer had a stern look about him. Straight away I wondered what the chemical formula was for urine as I thought I was going to piss myself! I remember he looked at us all and opened by saying, "For those of you who think that this might be an ideal opportunity to learn how to make explosions, high intensity thermite reactions or even polymer bouncing balls, you can forget it!" I thought "Oh my days - this guy takes no prisoners!"

For the first couple of weeks we did nothing but spend all our time, from when we started at 9.00am until we finished at 5pm, listening to the lecturers, making copious and lengthy pages of notes about what we were listening to, learning from the lecturers and also copying information down from the board. I had A4 pages upon pages of reference notes. I was thinking this is just unbearable. On a Wednesday, there would be an extra revision or catchup session from 5.30pm until 6.30pm.

Each lecture would last 45 minutes, and you would get a 15-minute break in between. I should point out that not all the lecture periods were taken by the tutors. In certain cases, you would get several study periods when you were required to carry on your studying on your own. If you chose not to take these opportunities seriously, and you got consistently poor marks in your homework or trials, then it was made clear that you would fail your exams. It was also made clear that, in order to pass, we had to do our utmost to listen, learn and absorb information.

I soon realised we were being treated more as adults than school children, as the onus and responsibility to learn and to do our own study sessions was down to us. No-one was going to make us do anything but, if you failed any course, you would only have only yourself to blame. Whereas in Secondary School it was more the responsibility of the teacher to make sure you achieved the right grades, sixth form college was a whole new world and a prelude to becoming an adult. The buck stopped with you in sixth form, if you mess up, that's your fault.

So began my introduction to college work. To avoid spending money that I really could not afford, I used to spend all my breaks, particularly at lunchtime, in the college library. In some cases, I was rereading stuff that we had gone through in class in order to try to understand it better while, in other cases, I was just trying to get my homework done. This was a totally new experience for me, the longer day, regular homework, self-motivation and the evening session on a Wednesday.

However, I found that, although it was hard and required a great deal of determination and concentration, it was very interesting. I'm not going to lie, I found it very challenging. Although the lecturers worked us hard, because they had all spent the larger part of their working life in industry before moving into the world of academia, we used to get some interesting stories. I know that some of my fellow students thought that they were distracting the lecturer in these lighter moments, but I quickly realised that it was very skilful teaching on the part of the lecturer. They would give us the impression that we were taking them off the subject but, suddenly, we were back on track and heads down again. I did, however, enjoy these stories as they showed what sort of career was potentially opening for me if I worked and studied hard.

After about a month of intense learning and stiff wrists from all the writing, we were taken next door into one of the three chemistry laboratories. This was such a great feeling. Here we were allocated a place where we were to work during our time in the laboratory. We were given our white lab coats and introduced to many other new pieces of kit that most of us had not dealt with before. This was going to be great! I thought my life was on the up.

But then the skies came tumbling down around my ears, my world came crashing down. The bubble burst! It must have been a Wednesday as I got home from college in the evening to find my mother in one of her increasingly common bad moods. I think my Mom and Dad had been arguing and I was about to get the backlash of her tongue.

"You needn't think that you can just spend your days lazing around in college, relying on me to feed and clothe you. You need to get a job and bring some money into the house; we cannot go on like this," my Mother barked. "You're the oldest and your Father and I cannot support you any longer!" she continued.

This was just the start and the pressure kept on mounting for about an hour or so. I tried to argue my corner to stand my ground but, in the end, Dad turned to me and said, "I am sorry, son but we cannot carry on like this. I cannot stand the constant arguments any longer." And with a sigh he said, "I am afraid that you will have to give up your college course and go and look for a job."

On reflection, I suppose that I was disappointed in Dad in that he hadn't stood up for me and allow me to continue my course. If he had, I now realise that my life could have been so very different and, like my youngest brother, I too might have ended up with a degree and a well-paid job. But, then, what did I know at that age? So, I went into college the next day, returned my books and told the office that I was reluctantly stopping my course. They were disappointed but, at the end of the day, it was my decision and I had to do it or face the wrath of Mother. I left the college in a mixture of rage, frustration, and disappointment. I had seen enough of the course to know that I could have done it and, more importantly enjoyed it, but now it was time to go out and to see what opportunities were open to me with my five "O" levels.

No rest for the wicked as my Mom used to say. The very next day, I went down to the main Job Centre in the centre of Birmingham and started looking for jobs. I had to first sign on with a Jobs Advisor, who started filling in a long form and asking all sorts of questions about what I wanted to do, what I was interested in and what I hoped to achieve. I felt like screaming at him and saying, "I know exactly what I want to do but I have been stopped by my Mother!" However, I knew how pathetic that would sound – a boy of 17 being totally dominated by his mother! What sort of jobs are best suited for me? Over the next few days, in fairness, he found me a couple of potential jobs with different companies, basically menial, underwhelming and poorly paid jobs that really didn't appeal at all as I didn't want to work outdoors.

Then my luck changed, a fluke maybe. I happened to be in the Job Centre and while browsing the job vacancy shelves, I spotted a new job that had only just been put on the display that morning; a local vacancy from an insurance broker that was seeking a "Trainee Insurance Technician" whatever that was! A technician in an Insurance company, maybe I had to change batteries or fuses or help with the maintenance? As far as I was concerned, however, the job had sold itself as it ticked all of my job requirements, local and office based.

I picked up the job vacancy card and took it to the Advisor, who immediately rang the insurance broker and got me an interview the following day. As I walked out of the Job Centre, I had a spring in my step but at the same time, but, I thought, what the heck do I know about insurance? The only dealings I have ever had was with the "Man from the Pru" who used to come around on a Friday evening to collect the weekly contribution to our household insurance. My only consolation was that it was a trainee position so I knew I would be given some training. I know that my Mom was pleased, as she made sure I was looking smart for my interview. I think she was more motivated than I was!

Chapter 6 – My First Job

To this day, I can still remember that first interview. I was very nervous and turned up, dressed in my best - and only - suit with a smart new tie and bright, shiny shoes. My interview was at 9.30am. I thought it was good practice to know a little bit about the company that you want to work for, so I had done a bit of research on the company before I turned up. I had phoned the day before on the pretext of buying insurance and, while getting a quote for my fictitious moped, I had enquired about what other types of insurance they did and how long they had been established, just a few basic questions.

I was so anxious not to be late for my interview that I arrived outside their offices at five minutes to nine. It was quite a large insurance broker that dealt with a range of insurances in the personal lines, non-commercial sector, for car, van, travel and household. So, I arrived, armed with at least something that I could talk to them about, I wanted to come across as competent and not a complete wally.

I walked into the office, which seemed to be filled with young ladies all busy at their computers. As I walked through the door, one of these ladies looked up, smiled and asked if she could help me. I explained that I had come for an interview for the position of Trainee Insurance Technician. She told me to take a seat and someone would come over to deal with me. I found a seat and picked up an insurance brochure off the table alongside where I was sitting and had just finished reading it when a well-dressed, suited man came over, introduced himself as the Office Manager and took me to his office.

He sat me down in front of a large desk. Also, in the interview was his Assistant Manager. She looked quite stern, in a head mistress kind of way, with large spectacle glasses. The Manager began by asking me about myself, what I had been doing since I left school and what I was hoping to achieve. He then went on to outline the details of the job for which I was being interviewed and said that, although I had no specific knowledge or experience of insurance, that would not necessarily rule me out.

I tried to answer their questions as honestly as I could although, at times, I might have stretched the truth a little to make me sound a bit better than I was feeling – after all this was my first ever experience of a face-to-face interview. About 30 minutes later, they thanked me for coming and told me to wait outside in the main reception area and showed me out. I was offered a drink and told to take a seat and they would give me an immediate decision in the next fifteen minutes, which I thought was potentially a good sign.

I kept my hopes high; I must have a small chance as I hadn't been told it was a definite "thanks but no thanks" but, honestly, I was just pleased to be doing an interview and getting some interview experience under my belt. Deep down, I never really expected to get the first job that I had applied for, that just doesn't happen to someone like me. I would have liked this job, though, as everyone seemed friendly and professional.

I was not looking for an outdoors type of job but was looking for a professional office job with a structured career path ahead of me – I was pessimistically optimistic! Thinking back, as I sat there, I felt that I had done quite well and had not embarrassed myself. Well I certainly hadn't disgraced myself for a young inexperienced teenager. Why would they tell me to wait? Surely that was a good sign as no one else was waiting here.

I was mentally going over all the questions and answers I had given in the interview when, after about twenty minutes, the Assistant Manager came out of the office and walked over to me; she explained that my interview had gone very well and they had done several interviews with a handful of candidates and I was the last one to be interviewed for this position. I was told the job was between me and one other candidate. This other person was older and had prior experience of the insurance sector, albeit only about six months and he had slightly edged it over me. She had discussed the two of us with the General Manager and together they had reached their decision. With that she apologised, thanked me for my time, wished me good luck and showed me out of the office. I was totally gutted. Was I downhearted? Yes of course. However, on the bright side I was happy to have just done my very first interview without making a fool of myself in a job sector about which I knew absolutely nothing. Too be honest, I was pleased with just getting the experience of an interview under my belt!

With that, I walked out and left the insurance office, weirdly still inside feeling a mixture of being deflated but upbeat, even though I didn't get the job and I remember that moment clearly to this day. I did something that was to have an impact on the rest of my life, I did a comedy euphoric jump in the air, clicking my heels in the air while doing so – in the similar style to an Eric & Ernie sketch! I thought to myself, "Well done me!" for doing a good interview and getting through it without making a total "numpty" of myself.

What I hadn't realised, nor could I have, was that my little 'clicked heels' routine had been witnessed and performed in front a large open-plan window. I had been in full view of all the ladies in the office who had watched me leaving and had seen me jumping in the air, even though I hadn't got the job, I still took the rejection well. If I had turned around at that exact moment, I would have seen about 10 staff at their workstations watching my show of jubilation. It had obviously melted their hearts because I had only walked to the nearest bus stop, about 50 yards from the office, where I was sitting waiting for my bus back home when one of the staff members came up behind me and called out my name and asked me back to the office.

My first thought was that I had left something behind. Unbeknown to me all the ladies had strongly voiced their opinion and rounded on the Assistant Manager and said that they wanted me to get the new job role instead of the other candidate and, as you know, the majority rule! To my utter amazement, the Assistant Manager told me that they had changed their mind (as the result of pressure from all the staff) and were prepared to offer me the job, starting on the following Monday at an annual salary of £4,750 - would I accept?

Would I accept? What do you think! I was over the moon. I could never have imagined that I would hit the jackpot on my first attempt at an interview and was shocked to realise that it was my antics of jumping in the air that had persuaded the ladies in the office that I was the "Trainee Insurance Technician" (affectionately called "The TIT") that they wanted to work with! There was no way that I could have imagined that such an impromptu jump in the air could have got me that job and, ultimately, put a stamp on how my life would change forever. I was working for the best insurance company I could ever have imagined; I have sometimes wondered whatever happened to the other candidate? – I feel sorry in some way that he never got to experience and have the same working highs as me and would never fully know the job he missed out on. He would have been truly gutted!

I could never have imagined what a wonderful, life-changing moment that was going to prove to be. From someone who had been robbed of the opportunity to follow his desired career path of going to college and qualifying for future positions in maybe the chemical industry, I had fallen well and truly on my own two feet, gaining a job in what looked like being the opening of a door into a completely new life. I was just 18, I was earning just over £400 per month, which to me was fantastic, and even after paying my Mom and paying off some bills, I was still left with over £40 in my pocket – I felt rich!

From day one, the staff there treated me as one of their own, I was part of a new family. They were so kind to me and generous with their time. They showed me how to do the various tasks but, obviously, as the Office Junior, I was also subjected to some pranks and leg pulling, all of which, I should hasten, were done in a sense of fun – it was just part and parcel of the day-to-day life in that office. To be honest, I really enjoyed it as it made me feel part of something for the very first time in my life. I felt that, not only did I fit in, but that I was liked for being me and I was not having to put on an act in order to make and keep my friends. This office building with all its employees was a like a new home with a new family, it was special.

I remember, on one occasion, I was told that my corporate name badge had arrived, I looked at the name on the badge "Sean O'Shea – Trainee Insurance Technician", I felt happy to be part of this team. I was told to make it official and, in order to get it all authorised, I was to take the badge to the Manager so he could sign off on it and to note it in the Employee Company folder. Now, I was extremely naïve and still very wet behind the ears. I strode purposefully over to the Office Manager in order that he could formally register the badge and present it back to me, rather like an army cadet being presented with a medal. So, suspecting nothing, I knocked on his door and explained that I had brought my new badge in order that he could formally present me with it. He looked a bit taken aback and must of thought "WTF!" However, he soon realised that I had been set up, as he saw about 10 pairs of eyes watching what was happening.

He stood there, taking it all in his stride and formally presented me with my badge, saying a few token words and told me to go and get on with my work. I walked out of his office feeling as proud as punch and it was not until I saw the grins on the faces of my colleagues that I realised that I had been well and truly set up. When I had recovered from my blushes and general embarrassment, I soon joined in the laughter, especially when one of the ladies brought me a cup of coffee as a gesture of their good-natured humour. Too be honest I never minded being the butt of the humour, as I took it with a pinch of salt. I was after all the newest and youngest office "TIT!"

Chapter 7 – Chalk and Cheese

Looking back on my working career, I can truthfully say that this first job was the best job that I have ever had. Like a drug, nothing compares to the first high you get; ever since, no other job has given me that same buzz! The working relationships, the fun, and the general camaraderie at that first job were something that I have never found elsewhere and, indeed, several office romances among the staff flourished.

What made it even better was that the fun and banter did not stop when the office closed at 5pm on a Friday. Every last Friday in the month, we would all go out together as a team and I can still remember the excitement among the staff as closing time approached on that day. In fact, you could feel the excitement in the office rising and building up gradually from as early as the 25th of the month. It was all we could talk about – what you were wearing, what time were we setting off, where we were going, where we were stopping after our night out, who's bringing a hairdryer on Friday – and that was just the lads' banter!

The men all got ready in one part of the office and the ladies in another. It was total chaos with everyone getting ready to go up town. We would all get on the bus, generally upstairs and all have a laugh – it was a great time as we all got on so well with each other. Those were great times. We would all eat too much, drink too much, dance too much and then collapse back at someone's house to sleep it off until the Saturday morning, generally waking up to the smell of coffee brewing and eggs, bacon, sausages, tomatoes, mushrooms and fried bread cooking – not that some of us actually felt like eating it after the night we had had.

Back at work, my immediate line manager was a single, older guy called Pat, and he reminded me of a combination of Alan Partridge and Phil Silvers, the actor who played Sergeant Ernie Bilko. He was a real character and a funny guy. He was supposed to be the person who showed me the ropes and to nurture and train me in the basics of insurance and a general understanding of policy wording. I was immediately taken by his dry sense of humour and his generally laid-back attitude. At the time, I would have been 18, young and naïve but eager to learn and he would have been in his early 30s. He knew the insurance business inside out, having done nothing else since he left school, but he lacked ambition and I believe that he was only there for the monthly pay cheque. He was very good at his job because of his years of experience and was a very popular member of the whole team. He was just happy to get on with whatever needed doing and let the rest simply flow over him.

I really liked Pat and he became like the older brother I never had. Like me, he was of good Irish stock and was a good guy to know. He always worked under the watchful eye of the Office Manager as, for the majority of days, he was late in to work (even though he lived the closest to the office) but, because he was so laid back and friendly with everyone in the office, this seemed to be tolerated. Pat and me quickly gelled as an individual team within the whole office structure, as he proceeded to show me the fundamentals of insurance and the paperwork required to set up an insurance policy.

He taught me everything about how to initiate cover and, also, how to make it look as though we were busy working when anyone came into our side of the office. We eventually became good friends outside work as well as drinking buddies. I was very fond of Pat and found his sense of humour and social company intoxicating. Our weekend drinking sessions would sometimes end up into the early hours of a Friday night and then in the morning the "hair of the dog" Saturday morning would continue on as another all-day session. The fun we had as drinking buddies would be some of the happiest times I knew and I will always remember them, well most of them. We also went on holiday together, leading my Mom to ask whether I was gay! That was Mom's way, she would come straight out and ask the direct question – not beating about the bush.

I remember once me and Pat and a few his friends were going to Gran Canarias and I was paying my deposit of the holiday by cheque only to realise at the last moment that I had only one cheque left in my chequebook, which I had written out previously but had forgotten to tear out and it had been left for a while and had slipped my mind. I showed it to Pat who said to sign the cheque over to the Travel Office and so I crossed out everything on the original cheque and put my initials everywhere, all over it and wrote over it again for a second time with the new beneficiary name, date and amount.

We were all in the travel agents, about eight of us, all handing our cheques over to the lady. I expected the travel agent to just accept my cheque and add it to the pile of other cheques collected but, when I showed it to her, she said that she couldn't understand a word written on it and, therefore, she wouldn't be able to accept it. I was utterly gutted and disappointed as I really wanted to go on holiday with them.

Pat looked at the cheque and could see I was really sad about the situation and agreed half-heartedly that, if I signed over the cheque again for a third time, crossing out the travel agents name and replace it with his own name he would pay my deposit. I just wish I had been there on the day that he tried to pay my cheque into his own bank account. The cheque was beyond deciphering, it should have been destroyed and must have been comical for anyone looking at it in Pat's local bank. Pat was a kind man with a good heart and I was proud to be his drinking buddy as he had a wide circle of friends to choose from, I felt pleased to be his "go to guy", especially after a hard day at the office.

The Irish population in Birmingham is huge but we all got to know each other and there was a great community spirit. Pat used to take me to the main Irish drinking pubs and clubs in the city and I was quickly accepted by his close circle of friends. I enjoyed their company and they seemed to enjoy mine and so we used to have some great nights out on the town, getting absolutely smashed out of our heads and ending up wasted in curry houses at around 2am, reading the menus upside down while trying to order food. Most times we would just end up with a takeaway as the restaurants just didn't want us being their problem.

On one of these evenings when I had been out drinking with Pat, I would have been about 18 and after I had dropped Pat off at his home in my car, I was at a bit of a loose end. It was around 10pm when a street hooker standing on a corner looked and casually waved to me. I thought why not, I was young and I felt that it was time that I found out just what it was like to have sex as I was still a virgin.

After a brief conversation and £20 changing hands, a very uncomfortable and awkward quickie ensued. It was terrible and the least romantic way to lose your virginity you could imagine. I greatly regretted it the moment it was all over but my regret was going to get worse. I got home and immediately had a hot shower but, then, after a couple of days, I realised that in return for the sex she had gave me a present of the crabs! My groin area was red raw and I was in agony! There then followed an awkward conversation with the local pharmacist when I asked for ointment to get rid of lice – "but not the lice for your head!" I said. The pharmacist knew exactly what I meant and without a further word she gave me the required ointment. That was a painful way to learn a hard lesson and one I kept very quiet about, until now!

A month or two later after the incident with the lady of the night I decided that the first time was a blip and I needed more sexual experience but this time I wanted to do it without paying for it. I needed help. I happened to be having a social drink with a work colleague and jokingly mentioned about my losing my virginity debacle and told him I was keen to put a line through the street hooker incident as quickly as possible.

"Have you heard of Joan?" he said with a smirk.

He then proceeded to tell me his mate knew of a middle-aged lady who lived locally who was in his own words open to casual hook-ups.

"Why not try knocking on her door and see what happens next?" he laughed.

He gave me her address and the following weekend I plucked up the bottle and decided to call round to her house totally unannounced and to see what would happen. I have this propensity to do things on impulse and to disregard or worry about the consequences later. This is no word of a lie. I was still 18 and was a little nervous but excited as I turned up on a sunny Saturday afternoon and knocked and rang the bell of this ladies' house. After a few moments of curtain twitching she opened the door slowly. My first impressions were positive, I thought she looked about mid 40's, quite slim, busty and attractive.

"Hi is your name Joan?" I asked with a bit of bravado and a cheeky red face

"Yes, it is" she replied.

"I'm sorry to bother you but I know a friend of yours and just wondered if you needed any gardening work doing?"

She looked at me for a few moments and then over my shoulder before saying, "Are you looking to do the garden today?"

I replied "Yeah, why?"

"So, where's your gardening tools then and are you planning on doing the garden in those clothes?"

I was wearing my grey work trousers and my Pierre Cardin pink jumper with a splash of my dad's Brut aftershave. I was momentarily at a loss as to what to say and hadn't really planned on doing any gardening or odd jobs for her and was starting to wish the ground would open up beneath my feet.

"I haven't got any with me!" I said with a bit of nervous bravado and a cheeky red face.

After a few more moments Joan said,

"You are letting in a draft, do you wanna come in for a cuppa tea then? Oh and what's your name?"

I just smiled lamely at her, told her my name and walked behind her as I followed her inside her home.

You may at this point want to know the salacious details of what happened next but I shall leave that up to your own imagination. Only to say I left about an hour later with the same slightly sweaty red face as the one I went in with.

Joan was an amazing lady and we met up a few times after that. I never kept in touch with her after those first few rendezvous but I will always have fond memories, bless her she was a good one, was our Joan!

I felt happy and was in good spirits I remember back at work I sought out my friend to thank him for passing on Joan's address to me.

One incident in the office with Pat sticks in my memory. He came in one morning, late as usual, and there was a huge pile of outstanding urgent and non-urgent post that had not been checked in or dealt with and had got to a level that it was deemed to be a major problem, as the post had built up over a week or two. It was not just our section, there were four sections in the office and there was a lesser, if not similar, situation with all of them, work had been really busy with new policies being signed up and the post had been put on the back burner.

This was back in the days prior to email when every correspondence was post and all cover notes were manual paper copies which were time consuming. The Manager called the section heads into his office and told them that we were all to work unpaid overtime until the backlog had been cleared. This was now a priority. There was a general groan from everyone, but it had to be done. The other three section heads devised a plan to bring their post back down to a manageable and reasonable level. Not mine, oh no, once the boss and all the other section leaders had gone home that evening, with everyone pushing to clear their backlog, Pat said to me with a wry smile, "Don't worry Sean" and in the style of Baldrick out of a Black Adder sketch said "I have a cunning plan!"

Pat turned to me and said, "Sean, I need you to sort this large box of post out into non-urgent, urgent, cheques and cover-notes" (cover notes provide temporary insurance until a full certificate is issued). Bear in mind that if customers are driving around with an expired cover note, then technically they are not insured if an annual certificate hasn't already been issued by the Insurer, so it is extremely important to make sure that everything is done properly. Cover notes are legally binding and important documents. These handwritten cover notes had to be written out precisely. If any of the other section leaders had been around and had walked in on us, they would have thought we were prioritising our workload. They might have even approved of our strategy and work ethic.

At the time I was a real newbie. I'd only been at work there a couple of months and I didn't really know the difference between a cover note, non-urgent and urgent post.

The office manager knocked on our door.

"You got this sorted Pat? He asked him.

"Yeah, we have a plan" Pat replied.

"Good, I will leave it with you to get this sorted, thanks for putting in the extra effort" he said.

To be quite truthful, I had a large box of paperwork which had no real semblance of order plus a separate pile of cheques, I was just staring at all this post for a good five minutes, then started going through it, piece by piece, letter by letter.

I said to Pat, "What time do you think we will have to work until?"

"Probs not too late" he replied.

"Oh, that's good, shall I further prioritise the post into date order so we work on the oldest first?" I asked

"Nah, no need to do that" Pat replied.

"Shall I keep back the cheques and put the hard stuff for you and the easy post for me?" I further enquired.

"Yeah, yeah, that'll be fine" he replied vaguely.

"Ok, I will crack on then!"

It was nearly seven o'clock by the time I had sorted through all the backlog of post and cheques.

Pat came over to see me.

"Sean, great job! Can you check that we are the last ones here?"

I told him that we were because I'd just come back from the toilet and all the other lights were off apart from ours.

He said, "Good, now that the last person has left the office, we are going to take everything, apart from the cheques and bin the rest!"

"You what! You're joking right?" I said

He went "No listen! Non-urgent stuff or even urgent stuff, the customer or insurer will write a second time if they haven't had a reply within a few weeks and we will just say we didn't receive your original correspondence!" That was his judgement call and to be fair he was probably right!

"What about all these cover notes?" I asked.

"Bin the lot, there will be a carbon copy and the annual cert on the client file!" he replied.

We put everything into two big black bin bags and went for a short walk down along a nearby canal, where we waited awkwardly until no one was around and dumped the large backlog of paperwork into a couple of bins along the canal and then we walked casually along the towpath. After we had ditched the paperwork we went for a couple of beers. Pat looked at me over a beer.

"Always think outside the box." He said with a smile.

I will never forget coming into the office the following morning to be met with a standing ovation – we had got the post from a huge bundle down to a few cheques! We had walked in wondering what was going to happen and instead we got a round of applause. Pat and I looked at each other - it was amazing but that was just the type of person that he was. If he could see a short cut to doing something, he would probably do it.

He said, "If it was really urgent, we will soon hear from the insurer, enquiring what is happening with regard to this particular policy, saying it was due to be cancelled and we would deal with it then!"

That was my best job ever in insurance, working in that company and, ever since then, insurance has been my fallback career choice but, sadly, no subsequent office job has ever been the same. Every time that I have worked somewhere else, I have always compared it with that job. The people there, with their characters, you could not recreate them. My life working for that company was glorious, it was the heyday of my working life. To be honest with you, I wish that it had happened later in my life when I would have benefitted more from the experience. At the time, I was young, I was naïve, I was gullible, but it was my initiation into office life. I just loved the people that worked there. If I could go back in time again it would definitely be 1986!

I met two other employees at this company who became close good friends and unbeknown to me would help shape my life and future. Obviously, no one has a crystal ball, unless you're a clairvoyant, but these two guys, Joe and Dave would eventually save my life. They were the exact opposite of me, they were smart, ambitious and were excellent at their jobs and, more importantly, knew and understood insurance better than anyone else.

Joe was like the office guru, if you needed some advice on an accounts query, you would go to Joe and he would help you, bearing in mind this was before the internet. Dave who was nicknamed "Three Files" because every time anyone saw Dave, he had the same three files tucked under his arm on the pretext he was busy, he was as sharp as a tack and knew the insurance systems and processes inside and out. If a policy had been issued incorrectly and needed amending, you would go to Dave and he knew how to sort out the problem. If a payment had been collected but not posted correctly, you normally asked either Joe or Dave to take a look. Both these two helped me whenever I needed it, if Pat was in a meeting or with a client. I was not jealous of them, I just admired them. They were of a similar age to me and we all got on well together. Joe would give me a lift into work each day in his yellow beetle car and Dave would help me out if I got stuck with a client with a problem at the counter, when I was on counter duty. We were like the three amigos. I enjoyed their company and we got on well together, probably as we were all lads in our late teens.

I stayed in that job for just over two and half years. Even though insurance was our core business I found that I had connected more with the people in the office than I did with insurance itself. It was the people and not the business that I loved, no one wakes up and says, 'today I want to work in insurance', it just doesn't happen that way. I must confess that I do get bored very easily and my life tends, therefore, to go in two-year cycles. Gradually, more and more of the people who were there when I joined the company and who had become my friends, left. Pat was offered a job with a large city Commercial Insurance broker, which whetted his appetite as he was getting bored with personal lines insurance. I was sad and gutted when Pat left as we had got on and bonded so well. Just like any family, people leave and move on to new pastures to experience new challenges.

With the change of personnel, it was inevitable that the social side would also change. Gradually, I fell out of love with the job and, to make it worse, Graham, the General Manager who had originally hired me, left to join another brokerage on the other side of the city – a better position and a better salary. Dave and Joe both got headhunted by a larger insurance broker. They both left and I was feeling more and more anxious. The company brought in more new staff to replace the old guard, but they were neither as nice nor as friendly and so the whole office ambience changed, and not for the better, I may add. My office family had moved on and I felt abandoned.

There was nothing unusual about this – people move around and change, nothing ever stays the same. Soon, I too also decided to leave to join another insurance broker. I thought I could find another insurance job with a better salary. I remember my second interview was in altogether different surroundings, in a local pub and he offered me the job on the spot and more money to leave. I enjoyed getting the attention from a prospective new employer, however this was a smaller company than my previous one, just half a dozen guys in an office and it was just work, work, work, with not a sliver of interest in any form of social life. They had financial deadlines to meet and we all had daily meetings to give us all an update on our individual sales, we were under constant pressure to hit our targets – it just was not the same and I certainly was not enjoying my daily working life as I had in the past. I found myself constantly comparing the two working environments – both brokerages were automotive and general domestic household – but the ambience and office banter were totally different - chalk and cheese!

Chapter 8 – Home from Home

I thought about moving into the commercial insurance sector, the same as my old mentor Pat. In the late 80's, it was very difficult to get into the top end commercial brokerage, you had to have passed all your ACII exams to even get your foot in the door. They only wanted the elite in the commercial sector. It's a lot easier these days but, back then, it was much harder. To get into commercial insurance brokering, you really had to know your stuff, so reluctantly I stuck to doing what I knew best and what I was familiar with, namely personal lines insurance - car, bike, home and travel. Consequently, because of all these factors, I fell out of love with insurance at this point in my life.

One evening, I was sitting in the pub with Pat, with whom I had met up with for a drink, we had stayed friends and we were just chatting generally when, suddenly, he turned to me and quite unexpectedly, said, "You aren't enjoying your new job are you? I can tell from your long face and the long silences that things aren't the same. When are you going to do something about it?"

This made me stop and think. If I was really honest with myself, I had been aware of this for some time, but I had needed this kick and nagging doubt from Pat to make me wake up and realise that he was right and that it was the time to move on.

"If you're not happy then find another job, you've got skills. Just don't bin post or extend cover notes past the renewal date!" he joked.

I had been in this second insurance broker for about months – it was closer to home and paid better, but it wasn't the same environment or the same people and so I wasn't happy and didn't enjoy the job anywhere near as much. I just wanted to leave. I felt stuck and didn't know what to do. I was still living at home with my Mom and the rest of the family, even though things were no way as near as bad as they had been previously with Mom, after all I was now bringing home enough to cover my boarding fees! I had in fairness been getting on a little bit better with my Mom of late, she was slightly amused and even laughed at a couple of my funny anecdotes; they made her chuckle and whenever we had friends around, she would always ask me to retell one such story:

I was going swimming and one day decided upon the idea of going to the top diving board about 10 metres up and looking over the edge to see how far up it was. I'm scared of heights and it was high up, it looked even higher up when you got there as you can imagine. I was up there minding my own business looking down, thinking this is mighty high up, when all of a sudden, I got asked by a few younger boys if I was going to dive.

"Excuse me are you really gonna dive off there?" one chirped at me.

Rather than just climb back down the stairs, I told them "Of course I'm going to dive. What do you think I'm doing up here? Admiring the view!"

They looked suitably impressed and, not wanting to disappoint them or look a coward, I turned back and made my run up and without so much as a second thought dived off the top board, headfirst into the pool below. They were creased up on the floor, crying with laughter at the loud bang and splash I made upon entering the water with some wer. I bruised my entire torso and legs badly. ad third degree burns! I was in a bad way but ember was those younger kids pointing and as I was being helped out of the swimming

Shortly after the 25th December 1989, I knew I had to find my own place. I came downstairs to unwrap a few presents, hoping to find a rather interesting gift. To my dismay, one of my presents was a small metal bin, the ones you pick up from the charity shop for 50p. I just stared at this small item for a few moments, this bronze tasteless waste paper bin and realised this was probably the worst present in the history of presents. No subliminal messages with Mom. I knew this was Mom's way of saying you might need this when you move out.

A week or so later, Mom was doing something in the kitchen, peeling some veg or putting some spuds on the boil, something like that and anyway I heard her say, "I'll help you find your own place."

"Oh, right, ok" I replied.

And that was that, she went and got the local paper from the newsagents and we started to look for cheap places to rent. We circled a couple of potentials and made a few enquiries. The very next day, I went with my Mom to try and find somewhere affordable to live. She was keen for me to try and fly the nest and get my independence and start becoming a man. She searched for the cheapest bargain-priced rooms to let and she shortlisted a couple.

The first one was a family mid-terraced home in a run-down part of town that was at my meagre budget level; it was already being lived in by a large family but they had a very small spare bedroom, with just enough space for a single bed, to the rear of the main bedroom. So, potentially, when I needed to go to my bed or use the bathroom, I would have had to creep gently and quietly, like some sort of intruder in the night, through the master bedroom, hopefully not waking anyone up. Not to mention the fact that it was a total mess and the whole house had a squalid, very lived in smell about it. I was not loving the idea of living in this slum. I remember turning to look at Mom assuming we were both on the same page. She looked at me with a stone-faced expression.

"It's perfect!" she said.

I could have laughed if I hadn't known she was being serious and, in the car on the way home, I told her in no uncertain terms that she was barking bat crazy if she thought I was moving home to live in that squalor. We also looked at another property that was in the 'red light' area of town, it was a small bedsit with a dreary single bed. It was the scummiest bedsit you could imagine and, again, my mother was upbeat about the facilities and glossed over the major problems as she tried to remind me of the positives, including an open-plan kitchen, a nice large window and a wardrobe. I mentioned to her that it had a shared toilet, there was damp on the walls, the few raisins on the floor were not actually raisins and there was a hole in the ceiling. It also felt as if someone had recently died there, it was not a homely place at all. It was utterly depressing!

Again, I repeated what I said about the first rental, that she must be mad if she thought I would move into this flea-ridden cess pit. It was obvious my mother was looking to get me out of the family home, so this pretty much made up my mind as to what I was going to do next. I had never been one for planning ahead financially and so I had virtually no money, I did not feel wanted or welcome anymore. Maybe I was outgrowing my home, I'd made new friends and I was going out more and more, then coming back late, normally drunk, so I probably was not helping my own situation or doing myself any favours. I would miss my Father and my two brothers, but I needed a new direction. I knew my time was up living at home and needed to fly the nest.

I decided that I wanted to leave both my home and my place of work. I'd made a mistake, a small blip on my C.V and couldn't stand working there, not even for one more day, I hated it. I knew my life needed a new direction and neither involved where I was living or working. I then had another argument with my Mother. I had been bringing home a decent wage and paying for my keep; she had received a call from my current employer asking where I was and why I hadn't phoned to let them know I wasn't coming in that day? They were obviously not impressed with me and neither was my Mom. After the argument, I went to my room and it was at this point that I made a firm decision- I had to go! I was going to leave home and to look for a new job. A new beginning - a new chapter!

Chapter 9 – Gold Pavements?

My Mother always shot from the hip; you always knew exactly where you stood with her. One night, shortly after our visit to the bedsit and after another argument, she said, "You just need to leave Sean, you're a man now and need to stand on your own two feet." She was very matter of fact about it.

"Yeah, I know Mom. I agree" I replied.

I had been thinking about leaving home more and more and I just knew that the sands of time had run their course and I had to leave. I was excited but nervous about leaving home. The tension at home was bad, it was becoming intolerable and I did not want my two younger brothers to experience this anymore, it was not fair to them or to my Dad. So, the next day, there was just Mom and Tom, who must have been about 9 or 10 at the time, in the home together and me upstairs. I packed the few things that belonged to me in my holdall bag and said my goodbyes, "I'm going. I've decided enough is enough and I'm off. I just can't live under this roof any longer."

There was no animosity, no emotion, no hugging. I was 19 and, despite having been in employment for over two years, I didn't have a penny to my name, I had spent it all in the pub or the bookies and I wondered how I was going to manage. Saving money was not something I was good at or considered important when I was a teenager. My youngest brother, Tom came up to my room and stood quietly for a few moments then with his arm extended, he said "Sorry you are leaving Sean, I've only a couple of pounds but you can have it" I was choked up that he gave me all his pocket money. I took it because I hadn't even the bus fare to get into town. I walked out of the house with a few clothes in my bag, my passport as ID and that £2 weighing heavy in my pocket. I looked back when I was about 25 metres from the door but it had already closed.

My plan, such as it was, was to hitchhike down to London and make my fortune on the streets that are paved with gold! Was I going to be the next Dick Whittington? Only time would tell, or so, they say. I remember to this day trying to hitchhike down the M6 motorway. It was obviously a difficult time, I didn't know whether this was the right route for me or even if it was legal, I didn't know if I was going to get runover. I felt like a pedestrian on a Formula1 racing track, the cars were just flying by at 70mph, only yards from me. This was January 1990; it was freezing cold and there were some patches of snow on the ground. Hitchhiking down to London seemed like a good idea at the time, apart from the fact I had walked for miles and that no-one picked me up because I probably looked a little bit out of place and people were increasingly wary of picking up solo male travellers, however after about three hours of walking with my right thumb raised up in the chilly air going numb, one kindly person finally did. I remember this van driver slowing and stopping, winding down his window and saying, "You can't walk down a bloody motorway mate! Where you off ta? I'm off ta London's Smithfield market if you wanna jump in."

"OK, thanks, much appreciated!" I replied, it wasn't as if I had been inundated with offers.

I thought to myself, is this stranger going to kill me or rob me? However, I realised shortly after we started on our journey that he was being a genuinely good Samaritan who just wanted the company. He took me to London and dropped me off at Smithfield Fish Market as promised, he said his goodbye and wished me good luck with finding my fortune! I spent the whole day asking fishmongers in the market for a job or just trying to find a job doing anything, but to no avail as either I was too late getting to the market or there were no jobs going,

I suddenly realised that it was approaching late afternoon and I had nowhere to go, no money, no-one to talk to and no friends. It was just a question of trying to work out what to do next. Being down in London on my own for the first and only time was very harsh because, if you don't know anyone, you are a nobody - it's an extremely busy but also a really lonely city; everyone has their own agenda and if you are not part of it you are ignored or simply rejected!

I suddenly had a reality check and it dawned on me I was royally screwed! London, like most capital cities can be a very intimidating and unfriendly place. I felt frightened and was totally out of my comfort zone. WTF am I doing here! The general population of London come into the centre for work and go home again. London is a very big city that is also very small, very community-orientated with the various villages and communities interlinked and spread around the centre. They tend to be very self-contained and protective of their own people. Consequently, if you do not know anyone and have nowhere to go, it is a very cold and lonely place. London can be whatever you want it to be, it can be a chic metropolis or a 24hour freak show, your choice.

What to do next? Here I was, too proud to admit defeat already less than 8 hours from arriving and go back to

Birmingham with my tail between my legs or do I remain to see another day in this unwelcoming city but with no foreseeable future – thrown out like the scrag ends and fish guts in the market where I had been all day! I had been here less than a day, it was way too soon to be contemplating throwing the towel in. If I did ever decide to return to London in the future, it would only be on my terms and only if I could show that the move to the capital was for my own benefit. This felt quickly like the wrong time and definitely the wrong place.

I remember that first night. I managed to find an old cardboard box and a doorway that offered at least some form of shelter from the weather. It was cold and hard and I found it difficult to get any sleep – there were lots of strange noises, people were on the move almost all night, I was hungry, I had a couple of pounds in my pocket, a bag with a couple of shirts, shoes and socks, a pair of trousers and some toiletries (job interview clothes!). I did not think about jumpers and warm clothes when I was packing! I was cold and gradually beginning to get wet as the rain began to pour down. I tried as best I could; I used the socks as gloves, my bag as a pillow and the cardboard box I opened and used as a ground sheet, I turned away from the pedestrians to face the doorway. I was humiliated and kept thinking that 24 hours earlier I was sleeping comfortably in a nice warm bed, how different a single day can make.

I didn't want anyone to see me scared and crying. I had only been in my own little doorway for what must have been just a couple of hours, but which had seemed longer, when this scruffy Scottish guy came along and told me that I was sleeping in his space! He stunk of piss. I was sober and he was drunk, he was not a polite drunk, he swore and threatened to beat me up if I didn't fuck off! I told him the police had already told me to move along. The words police must have sobered him slightly as he went on his way without another word. That set my nerves on edge and, after he had staggered on his drunken way, I tried to settle but every noise and footfall set me wondering what was going to happen next. I don't think I slept a wink!

Chapter 10 – McDonald's Saved My Life

Over the next few days, I wandered around the streets, minding my own business and doing a lot of people-watching and loads of thinking, coming to the hard realisation that London was not paved with gold but rather dirt, mud and rubbish, oh and more dirt! My brother Tom's pocket money had long since been spent and I was now walking the streets looking for dropped coins. I felt dirty, depressed and desperate. I'd been in full time employment until recently and now I was treasure hunting for gutter coins! The streets were inhabited by a strange, but constantly changing, group of people, a minority of whom were friendly but mostly the majority of whom were agitated, angry and stressed. Drugs and alcohol seemed to be the main replacement for food.

One thing that I learned very quickly, having just avoided an altercation with a drunk Scottish homeless guy, was to treat everyone with suspicion, as I never knew how they might react. I was young and plum pickings for any unscrupulous stranger. To be fair, I did find some kind, friendly souls who were interesting to talk to and who explained their own story and reasons for ending up on the streets, but they were few and far between. It made me realise just how bad life could get if you were not in a job or in a wholesome family environment. No one is born on the streets, no one wants to live there, it is literally rock bottom and a lot of people I met did not deserve to be there. Some homeless people might have previously led a normal, totally unscathed life had they not been made unemployed through no fault of their own, been in a violent relationship or even been physically or sexually abused. Our Government, and society in general, should not forsake these individuals and should try harder. More help should be given to people living on the streets, we are not a third world country, we are one of the richest nations on the planet. It's tough on the streets and it is no life at all.

I now had lived rough for a while in London, maybe a month or so. I had not been begging for food, but I was stealing a few groceries to survive. I was told once that retailers and shop keepers put the price of merchandise up to compensate for theft, just like insurance companies increase premiums because of claims. I was not going to put a shop out of business by taking a sandwich or can of pop, I was balancing out the economy. I used to shoplift only for food, I'm not proud of that fact but I wanted to live, I needed to survive as I always felt I didn't belong in the gutter. I also didn't want to go through the extreme humiliation of going back home a total failure. I had only been down there for a short time and I wanted to go back and be able to show my family, especially my Mom that I had made something of myself.

It was very difficult living rough, however, eventually, I struck lucky, well as lucky as one can be when they are living rough in London, when I found a 6-foot long, metal 3-drawer filing cabinet on some derelict wasteland. I made this piece of office stationery my living quarters for a couple of months. I literally slept in a metal coffin! It was very difficult a first, as you can imagine, for it was very cold at night. I must have had some resilience I thought, and, just maybe, shown a shred of ingenuity. I laughed and remember thinking that one day this would make a good story. I took out all the filing drawers and turned it on its front, so the drawer's space was facing the ground and crawled into the metal filing cabinet for warmth and a little bit of comfort.

It was coming into Autumn now, and the nights were getting longer and colder. I hated every moment of it. I was still just nineteen years old; I had no prospect or future and I was living rough in an unwanted cold, vandalised rusty old filing cabinet. At this very moment in my life I felt I could not get any lower, my self-esteem and my determination to succeed seemed to have evaporated, and only my pride and vanity to see through just one more day remained, something good must surely happen to make things better. I did a lot of praying. I remember that I prayed for forgiveness for stealing the food, I prayed for upsetting my family and I prayed for God to show me a path, any path. I could see no light in my filing cabinet. I was struggling both physically and emotionally and felt like I was living my life apart from everyone else, I felt totally and utterly isolated. I was unloved and abandoned.

This was my life – it was hard, cold and it was lonely. I could see that, if I didn't get out of it quickly, I could be trapped for life, just like so many of those amongst whom I had lived. Looking back in years to come, it made me realise that, while it had been hard, it has perhaps made me much of the person that I am today – living on the streets, living rough, being homeless and generally looked down upon and treated like dirt by many of the people around me. We were the forgotten many. One single kind gesture remains in my mind. I woke up one morning when I wasn't in my "Chez Filing Cabinet", I remember I was in the doorway of a large commercial building and woke to find that someone had placed a black trilby hat on my head during one particularly cold night – a small gesture by that one single, solitary person, that one act of kindness, I will always remember.

It also made me realise that, in general, the main mass of people could not give a damn about who or what you are, what your background story is, we were just a group of people to be ignored and stepped over. It's so sad that, in many cases, these people have had a bad turn in their life which has dropped them into this new life and, for many, it has not been their choice but simply where they have ended up because they had nowhere else to go nor anyone to help them. Finally, it made me realise that this was a way of life which I wanted to get out of as quickly as possible before it sucked me in and killed me.

To this day, if I walk past a homeless person, I always give them some change or exchange a few words as I know how it feels to be on the receiving end. So many low points but I was not a worthless cause just yet, but I knew that I had to do something and that I needed a job fast, but I did not know how, where or what to do next to find employment.

However, at that time in the early 90's, McDonald's restaurant was doing a special offer a "No purchase needed scratch card" where you could go in, collect a scratch card from the assistant behind the counter with no purchase necessary. The card had a simple question with a scratch-off answer, if you got the question right, you would win whatever food prize was underneath the winning answer. I remember my day-to-day existence revolved around going to different McDonald's and getting various scratch cards trying to get the question right to get myself a portion of fries or, if I was lucky, a burger and that was how I existed, which was obviously very harsh, very hard and very true. I now look back on those days and I suppose they made me what I am today, because I realise now that the other side of life, living on the streets, living it rough, being homeless was something that I never ever wanted to experience again.

One day I was in the toilets in McDonald's with just two 2 pence pieces in my pocket that I had found and I remember washing my face and armpits in the sink and trying to pull the hairs out of my face and chin to try and make myself look more presentable, because I knew that I was looking more and more like a down and out, a homeless bum! I just needed to look presentable enough to get a scratch card in the first place and look as though I had money in my pocket. First impressions are invaluable. I could call myself a bum because that's how I felt about myself. I stank, I looked as though I had aged about ten years and I felt worthless, but I always had to look presentable enough for the assistant behind the counter.

I always went to the restaurant toilet first to spruce myself up before I ever went to the counter. I was tired, I was lonely, I was depressed and probably wasn't much to look at because, quite honestly, I was feeling like a hobo - I had only one clean albeit creased interview shirt and pair of trousers to my name. I was in a bad way and a worse place. This was not what I had planned with my life, how on earth had it gone wrong so quick.

Then, one morning while enjoying a burger that I'd just won, I just happened to start talking to another guy at the long sit-down high stool window table in McDonalds. It was a pure fluke, but this guy sat next to me, he didn't judge me for looking a little rough and tired around the edges and he struck up a conversation with me. I felt so pleased to engage in the most basic of human functions. We began general chit-chatting about life in London, how he was not liking the weather. He said he had recently come over from Poland, he had been living over here for a month or so and was missing his home town of Krakow, but he had found a better paid job over here as there was hardly any well-paid work back home. His English was a lot better than my Polish.

I was interested to find out what he had done; how had he managed to find a job when he had only just come over from Poland? How had he landed on his feet so quickly and he didn't even come from the UK? He said that he had found a job working in a local city pub.

I said, "That's nice, well done on securing a job, which Pub?"

He said, "London pubs give you food and bed for free!"

It was a lightbulb moment! I said, "Really – you get accommodation and food when you are working in the pub?"

He said, "Yeah, it's very true. Rooms too expensive to rent, so get them with job."

"I didn't know that!" I replied.

Well, I was dumbfounded as I had not realised Central London licenced premises offered this kind of arrangement. It was their way of recruiting staff, as the cost of living was so high in London that this was a great way to secure employees. So I developed a battle plan, an employment strategy for the next day, to smarten myself up and find a bar job. I made a real conscious effort to make sure that I had the best appearance that I could muster and a believable cover story as to how and why I wanted (desperately needed!) a job in the pub trade. I had my back-up shirt, trousers and shoes for this very occasion. I made myself as presentable as possible and with a quick pitstop at my local

McDonalds for some fries and a freshen up I began my search for employment with a spring in my step. I spent all day walking around the streets of London, going into loads of pubs, asking if they had any jobs. I was just blagging my way really. They asked me where I was from and what I was doing? I explained that I had come down to London only in the last couple of days and had been working in the pub trade up north and tried to blag my way into a job. At the end of the day, when I had approached about 15 or more pubs, I found one job where the manager was a grumpy old guy who chatted with me for about 15 minutes then out of the blue just came out and said he would take a punt on me and, in his words, "I'll chance my arm and give you a trial son, but don't mess me about or you're out!" If I turned up, I could start the next day. I was totally overjoyed and felt on cloud nine, I had a new job which offered accommodation as part of the job. That was a real relief, knowing that I had somewhere that I could stay at night and, to be honest, I don't think I slept a wink on my last night in the filing cabinet!

I learned and picked up the pub trade quickly. Having said that, the salary was very poor but, if you add in the fact that I was given free food and lodging, then, overall, it really was not too bad, considering the location. I was working directly opposite the London law courts. I had been homeless and now I had a new home. I wouldn't moan, I was just happy to be of value to someone and feel human again. In total, I spent nearly six months there and it did enable me to get back on an even keel both mentally and financially. I was able to eat regularly and while I did drink sociably, after shifts, with the clerks, lawyers and other punters who worked in the Law Courts nearby, I was able to save some money and even able buy some new clothes so that I looked the part. I must admit I did scrub up well.

You had to get up very early in the morning and you had to learn how to pull pints properly – obviously, initially, I had no idea how to do it. I was given some basic training by some of the bar staff and slowly but surely began making my way – learning how to pull a decent pint and how to make decent banter with the punters. It's not as easy as it looks, as some breweries are really proud of their cask ales and, if you don't pour the beer properly, if the nozzle is too tight and it comes out to quick or too frothy, then the punters will just moan and grass you to the manager. I was determined to do a decent job. It was an apprenticeship in learning how to pour pints. I learned quickly, got on well with it and it was the banter with the customers that I enjoyed as much as anything. It was a regular job, and everything just seemed to fall into place. I loved it and had made some friends with the locals and really looked forward to talking with some of the clerks from over the road. They earned a huge wedge of cash each month for sorting the administration out for the Lawyers. They were rolling in it and weren't afraid to splash the cash in the pub.

However, as I had already found to my dismay, good things do come to an end and it never lasted, not for me anyway! After a particularly quiet trade period, business was bad. I was advised that, as I was the last one in, I would be the first one they had to let go. My employment would end in a couple of weeks at the end of the month. I had done nothing wrong, but the overheads meant the landlord couldn't afford to keep me on the payroll. I pleaded for him to reconsider and said I would do whatever he wanted me to do, however his mind was made up and there was no changing it.

I became complacent over the final two weeks of my employment. I wasn't getting up on time to clean and set up the cellar correctly. I was tired because I had been spending a lot of my time after work drinking and propping up the bar with the regulars. The air was coming out of my balloon and I didn't care as I knew I was leaving and I just thought, "fuck it!". I had lost my mojo and wasn't bothered about doing the job I was being paid to do. I also admit at this point to taking money from the till to line my pockets and to give myself free drinks when no one was around. There was also a large 6 litre whiskey bottle that was used to collect change that stood proud at the back of the bar. It had been there years and was part of the fixtures and fittings. As there was no CCTV, I thought nothing of getting that heavy bottle down one morning before my shift was due to start in order to unload about £100 worth of pound coins.

Now I know that this was despicable and I'm certainly not proud of this fact, but I need to be as honest as I can in order to tell my story, and that includes all the stuff I regret. I thought I needed to look after myself as I was going to need all the money I could get once I left this job and no-one was going to give me a free handout. I felt entitled to do this as I was being given the boot and in London it really is dog eat dog! I knew this was wrong, but I didn't want to leave, and I was feeling down about the thought of what might happen to me. I was disappointed to be leaving some new friends I'd made over the last 6 months or so. However, even though I was gutted, I realised this was another stepping stone and an opportunity to see what life had in store. Even though I was being made redundant I had learned a skill and saved up a few quid. I was still in a better position than I was 6 months earlier.

By chance, during my last couple of weeks while working in the pub, I got talking to a small group of people from Belgium who had been over to England for a holiday and were soon to return home to Brussels. There were about 4 or 5 of them, all students with varying ages from about 20 to 30 years old. They came into the pub a few times over the last week that I was working there. They were stopping in a local hostel while they were sightseeing. I mentioned that I was leaving at the end of the month and one of them, Sophie, said I should go to Brussels as it was a vibrant city and was a great place to live. It had loads of restaurants and bars and a museum dedicated to "Fries". They said I could probably get a job straight away as I was living in the EU and I had experience of working in a pub. I thought the prospect of a new country and new place was exactly the new start I needed. I jotted down the Sophie's address who said I could crash a night or two at her place if I ever got over there. It was the end of 1990, and 1991 was around the corner. A new year and a new life, who knew what the opportunities that were waiting for me in Belgium, I was now excited.

How wrong I was, 1991 was going to be a year to forget!

Chapter 11- Becoming an Immigrant!

My last shift could not come quickly enough. I had my bag packed, my money safely hidden away with my passport and I was nervous to be travelling to a new country. I called home for the last time and remember speaking to my Dad, he asked me how I was keeping and said he was pleased to hear from me. He told me he had only just recently lost his own father. My Grandad had got run over whilst on his pedal cycle in Ireland, he was out shopping one day when a hit and run driver had knocked him off his bike and killed him instantly. It hit me hard as I really loved my Grandad, we had a special bond and with him dying I told my Dad I was going to be travelling abroad and would not be in contact for a while but just wanted him to know I was alive. I wished I could have said more to him but I was just distraught about learning the news about my Grandad. I left Britain not realising that I would not be talking to my family for the next four years or more.

I caught the ferry across to Ostend and then the train to Brussels. I was still reeling after finding out about my Grandad, I felt so hollow and empty inside. However, upon arriving my mood instantly changed, my first thoughts of Brussels when I arrived was this place was *"Wow, this looks so cool and funky"*. The train station walls were adorned with large professionally done graffiti murals. Outside there was a cool breeze blowing. I knew that my priority was to look up Sophie and to get a roof over my head.

Brussels is very modern and has a chic cosmopolitan vibe to it. I began to walk and to soak in the atmosphere.

The architecture and buildings are huge - it has an immediate impact. I remember walking past the busy coffee shops, they were just bustling, full of people drinking and chatting in a multiplicity of different languages. Brussels has lovely long, wide roads, the place was a beautiful picture and deceptively pretty. I think my arrival in Brussels must have coincided with it being a Thursday evening and one of the busiest social nights of the week. A lot of people travel short distances from France, German and the Netherlands weekly for the weekend festivities. The bars were packed with well-dressed people sitting outside drinking coffee and sipping beer.

Place de Luxe is one of the busiest parts of the city with a square block of bars and cafés, the patrons arrive and merge on to the large courtyard to relax and unwind. Brussels is a true definition of a European City, not only since it is a major visitor attraction as well as being a centre for business, government and international trade.

The smells from what seemed to be a myriad of cafés and bars of all nationalities wafting out as I wandered past were excruciating! In the end, I did yield and have a coffee and a bun but had to restrain my urges to invest in a meal, despite all the temptations! I sat and admired what I learned was the Royal Palace which, when fully lit at night, was truly amazing sight. My first impressions were that I thought Brussels was just wonderful. After stretching out one coffee and a choux pastry bun for as long as I could, I decided to try and find and locate Sophie's apartment. I was relieved to find out that the street Sophie lived on did actually exist as part of me had wondered if she had written down a correct address after travelling over 200 miles.

When I arrived, I was exhausted and tired but happy to have found the correct location and to see Sophie's name listed.

I first heard it about halfway up the stairs to the apartment, there was a lot of noise. To be exact a lot of shouting, arguing and screaming. I soon realised this noise was emanating from behind Sophie's door. I decided after a long pause to knock on the door. The shouting soon stopped, and a tall middle-aged man opened the door and looked me up and down. I was frozen to the spot as Sophie arrived a few moments later behind him, she had mascara and makeup running down her face, she was obviously emotional and there I was just standing there with cream around my mouth from the bun I'd just consumed and a packed bag over my shoulder. I did not know what to do and just stared like a rabbit in the headlights at this man who was undressed from the waist up.

Sophie did not immediately recognise me but after a moment or two she kind of smiled and looked sheepishly at me. The large guy said something in German and went back into the room.

"Is this a bad time?" I asked

"I'm so sorry, Steve, but you could not have picked a worse time," she said, obviously not remembering my name. "You should have phoned before you arrived," she continued.

"I'm sorry, you only gave me your address" I replied sheepishly.

"I'm leaving here in the next few days to return back home, I'm really, really sorry but I have to deal with my shit," she said.

There was more loud shouting from the German guy back in the apartment and with that she said goodbye and quietly closed the door and left me standing there for a few moments, totally bewildered and in shock.

I was stranded in a large unknown city and there was no big master plan! I didn't do a lot of forward thinking in those days - I had a "day to day" philosophy and I was living on a wing and a prayer. I was young, I had some money but I didn't want to spend it all on accommodation as that would eat into my funds quicker than a coin toss and so I ended up sleeping rough – again! What was I to do?

Over the next couple of days, I tried knocking on a few doors to get a pub job again but I struck out as I did not have any work permits or visa. I was drawing a blank getting a job and was getting déjà vu. I was doing the same thing again, just a different county with a native language I couldn't speak a word of. I was even more lonely and stranded and feeling cold and constantly thinking about food. With hindsight I probably should have just got back on the first train back to London, but that would have seemed like going backwards and seemed a bit of a defeatist attitude and I wanted to see where my own adventure would take me.

Then my luck changed - or so I thought. I happened to bump into Pierre whom I had met in London. He asked me what I was doing and when I explained what had happened since I left them in London, he said, "Why don't you bunk down tonight at my place and then we can see what is on offer?"

I quickly agreed and after stopping to get some food for that evening and for breakfast, we went to his flat, which turned out to be in the centre of Brussels and which had three bedrooms and a couple of large, soft couches. We cooked a meal, which we washed down with some beer that he magically produced. We then settled down to some weed until about 2am, when we caved in. The following morning, after breakfast, we set out to see who we could find of Pierre's friends. He knew where they were likely to be and, sure enough, we found a gang of them in one of Brussels' many parks. He introduced me to Jan, who seemed to be the one with the local knowledge of the night life scene and, apparently there was a party that evening at Jan's flat, starting around 7.30pm. We sat around for a while and then we decided to split up and meet back at Pierre's around 7pm, where we agreed that we would have something to eat before partying!

Never having been to Brussels before, I decided to have a wander around the city centre. It seemed to be a huge modern city with lots of ancient buildings in between. Obviously, since it was also a major visitor attraction as well as being a centre for business, government and international trade, there seemed to be a myriad of cafés and bars of all nationalities and the smells wafting out as I wandered past were excruciating! In the end, I did yield and have a coffee and a bun but had to restrain my urges to invest in a meal, despite all the temptations! After stretching out one coffee and the bun for as long as I could, I decided to continue my wandering until it was time to head back to meet up with the others.

Back at the flat, two things were noticeable. First, the numbers were swelling quite rapidly and second, there was a definite smell of drugs. We were welcomed in and I was introduced to a great number of people, most of whose names I would not remember, not that it mattered, and I doubt if many remembered or cared about me. Before I could say anything, a glass of beer was put into one hand, and a joint in the other.

"Get that into you," said Annette, one of Pierre's friends. "Just relax and enjoy yourself."

I decided to have a look around the flat and, I was initially surprised to see at least one couple enjoying themselves on the floor and on Jan's beds. Suddenly, I felt an arm around me.

"C'mon, darling," came this slurred voice, "Don't just stand there, come and talk to me." With that, she pulled me to the floor and cuddled up tight, before I could react. For the next few hours, the memories became more and more hazy as the combination of drugs and alcohol took over. At least I was able to forget about England, work and debts for a while. I must have dropped off to sleep because the next thing I remember was that it was daylight and there was a smell of coffee on the brew. I looked around, to find that I was not the only one who had kipped out or collapsed on the floor by the end of the party. I got up and staggered to the bathroom, was violently sick, and found my way to the kitchen where I tried to get my way through a strong, black, Continental coffee.

This was to be my introduction to the drugs and party set in Brussels and we went from house to house for over a week, partying every night. I do not know where the money for the drugs and alcohol came from, but they never seemed to be in short supply. However, like all good things, they had to come to an end. After about a week of constant partying the group decided that they would each go their own way and so I was left to find a new way forward on my own.

To be fair, we had had some good nights out, parties and stuff like that When the parties stopped, however, I was all alone, with nowhere to stay and so I ended up spending all my time thinking what to do next. I was in Belgium; I was stranded and there was no big plan! I didn't do a lot of forward thinking in those days – I was living on a wing and a prayer. I was young and I was sleeping rough – again! Homeless and hungry I realised I was going to have to sleep rough, I knew that before long something would happen or an opportunity arose, it normally did. However, in the meantime it was back to sleeping rough until something happened.

What was I to do? I wandered around the streets of Brussels for several days, sleeping in doorways and in whatever shelter I could find. I looked through my bag of clothes that I had brought with me from London and selected the oldest and most tatty clothing I could find which, by this time was not difficult and, in the time honoured tradition of begging, set up a piece of cardboard in front of me bearing the plea in French "Britannique, Faim et Sans-Abri!" ("British, Hungry and Homeless!") – I copied this from a sign that I had seen in front of another street dweller, in another part of town.

Brandishing a battered plastic bowl, which I had found in a bin and which I hoped would soon be resounding to the sound of money, I found a place on the cold pavement and put myself at the mercy of the good folk of Brussels. Blessedly, it wasn't very long after I'd squatted down at my chosen (and particularly uncomfortable) pitch – the old working-class district at the foot of the city's Palais de Justice - that coins, albeit of the small denomination variety, started rattling into the bowl.

Against the sound of metal hitting plastic, I had to pinch myself to remember that I was being given money by total strangers for doing nothing other than looking rather pitiful and desperate. A short time later, a woman bent down, dropped a couple of coins in the container and said, in

French, and then in English, "If you are round here later, you can come to me for your dinner." Kind though it was, I didn't go. However, the kind-hearted woman, who must have been in her 70s, had dropped five coins into the bowl. A small amount, yes, but it's the thought that counts, as the saying goes – it also bought me something to eat!

Another passer-by directed me to the nearest shelter for homeless people and asked if I would like some toiletries. She burst into tears as she was saying it. Soon afterwards, a young woman said she had no money to offer but, instead, asked if I wanted some warm clothing. Then, after what seemed like an eternity – but what was, in fact, only about 35 minutes - without attracting the slightest interest, a man touched me on the shoulder and offered me a pair of socks. I thanked him and he replied saying, "Don't stay in the cold too long."

On another day, and by way of contrast, my next stop was just off the Chaussée de Waterloo in Waterloo, just a few kilometres from my previous spot. I was now at the centre of an enclave for rich commuters and expats. It's an area where, even then, it was not uncommon for properties to swap hands for over €1million and, unlike the previous pitch, a part of the city that simply oozes wealth. Fertile ground for begging, you might think. However, I found that for all the relative kindness shown to me by people in the previous spot, the majority of those in Waterloo barely turned their heads in apparent indifference when they passed me by.

One man shouted that he wasn't going to give me anything "because you are going to spend it on drugs." Many people on the streets are not only homeless but experience mental illness and/or addiction issues but, I wondered, did he really think that's what I would have done with whatever pittance he may have offered? Many people seemed desperate to avoid eye contact, let alone offer any words of comfort. Time dragged by like an eternity and it was painful and noticeable just how slowly the cash trickled in. It was also here that I encountered my only particularly aggressive and negative reaction. A burly man pointed to my pathetic little sign and shouted at me, "Trouvez un boulot" (it roughly translates as "Find a job"). If only I could, I thought.

After nearly another two hours huddling in the winter chill, I counted out the money from my Waterloo takings. I'd been given the rather measly sum of 10 Belgium Francs, compared with 50 Francs in central Brussels. Having spoken to some other street dwellers, one offered to let me crash on his "pad", an old mattress that he'd installed in a doorway. Basically, though, I would spend the days walking miles around the city

There were a couple of times where I went into a hostel for homeless people. They tended to be in older buildings in the poorer part of Brussels, but they offered, typically, 20 bunk beds and a café area. The big advantage, however, was that you could go in and have a shower and get cleaned up. You could even do your washing – what little I had after all this time! I remember visiting a couple of homeless hostels, but, in general I would walk for miles around Brussels without any plan.

Since those awful days, the city has done a lot to help the homeless with more than 1,200 hostels staying open at night throughout the winter to remove all the homeless from the streets. Today, the majority of the estimated 1,000 people who spend their nights in these hostels are men, but some are also women with children. In addition to providing food and shelter and bathing facilities, these hostels are now offering medical and psychosocial support to gradually wean more of them off the streets. However, when I was struggling there, there was none of this help available.

Things had changed rapidly, parties were no longer happening, and I realised that I was on my own again. I didn't know what to do next. I had lost touch with the friends that I had met up with, I didn't have a mobile phone, I didn't know what I was doing, and I suddenly realised one day that I was back to square one again. What do I do? Do I go back to London and get my old job back? Or do I find out where life now leads me?

I had tried on several occasions to obtain bar work and would walk in off the street and see if there were any vacancies, but each time I was asked to show my official proof of residency and documents to confirm I had permission to work. I was an illegal immigrant and had no legal status.

This is no criticism of Brussels but, just like any other city and a major international one at that, they are cold and lonely places to be if you do not know anyone and do not have anywhere to stay. It also does not help when you are on limited funds, as I was desperately trying to eke out what money I had left for as long as possible. At my lowest point, and one I was most embarrassed about, I used to find quite a profitable doorway right next to a street bin approximately 100m from two adjacent fast food places near the centre of Brussels and watch the people leaving with their containers of hot food and, hopefully, if I'd got it right, by the time they reached my bin they would dispose of the remnants of their container. I thought of it as just like sharing food. after all sharing is caring! After all some people eat roadkill, so this was just warmed up roadkill in a container.

One of the major problems that I quickly faced was how to generate cash. My own funds that I had brought from England were low and looking bleak. I had kept some on one side as a contingency fund but, for my current day to day living, I was struggling and was becoming increasingly desperate to create a new source. I did have one idea and one day, after a shower in a hostel and wearing my best clothes, I walked, bag in hand, purposefully into a Commercial Business Development Centre in the middle of Brussels and asked for an appointment with a business adviser. I was put in front of a little old Belgian gentleman – smart suit with a brown bow tie. He asked me straight away in English, without any pause to determine whether I was any other nationality, to outline my business idea. I explained to him that my idea related to providing a temporary storage locker facility at railway stations, airports and shopping retail outlets. There would be a set of lockable, wall-mounted cabinets of different sizes, where bags, luggage or shopping could be stored safely for short periods of time for a small fee at popular venues and shopping retail outlets. I asked him what he thought of the idea and his response overall was in general, quite positive.

"Give me your full name, contact information, your business plan, details of your permanent place of residence and then we can see what we can do to help. Oh, and do you have all the required legal permits?"

Of course, I had none of these and so, having wasted about 20 minutes of his time, I was shown the door. This was my goal at the time – to find a niche market and make the money come pouring in but I was like a goldfish swimming round amongst much bigger fish and floundering out of my depths in all aspects. I was a lost soul, I just needed to get a foot in the door or even just a small step on the ladder. I felt like I was drowning and just separated from normal society, no viable opportunities were presenting themselves to me. I remember feeling that, as I had had nothing in the UK, I would try and see what the rest of the world had to offer. I was young and wanted to experience life beyond the constraints and walls of the UK. I was not aware at that time that my fictitious walls were all too soon going to be replaced by real ones. I had wanted to get out of the UK as I had felt that it was quite restrictive, not realising what the future held for me. So far, Belgium had not seemed to be the answer to my prayers – or my hopes and dreams.

One night, while I was walking the streets of Brussels, I had nowhere to stay and was walking along a canal towpath; it was late at night and the temperature was very cold and frosty. I was freezing cold. It was at that moment that I spied an old, somewhat fair-weathered canal boat that was not in the best condition. It was a freezing cold night and the boat looked as though it was not being used, so I decided to sleep on board this narrowboat, which was tied up at the side of the canal. It had a fragile lock on the cabin door which came away with a small pull – it was going to be the place where I laid my head that night. I remember thinking that this was alright for a sleepover for a night, but I was extremely conscious of falling asleep, only to be wakened by the owner giving me a punch or a kick for breaking into his little boat. Then, to my surprise and delight, I found, in one of the cabinets at the end of the bed, a half bottle of Scotch. I drank straight from the neck and it instantly warmed and settled me. In no time I was chilled out and snug in my little dwelling. I slept soundly for about six hours until, bleary eyed, I was woken by the dawn chorus and got up, made the single bed tidy again and put the bottle of scotch back into the cabinet and left the little warm snug boat the way I found it.

I left first thing, at the crack of dawn, as I did not want to tempt fate nor to be seen by any of the other canal boat dwellers. I realised that finding a warm safe dwelling in the city was going to be impossible, I knew my options were limited and it was at this point that I realised that Belgium was not going to offer me a great deal of opportunity. I was obviously not carving out a living or establishing myself in Belgium. I was an immigrant living in a foreign county with little money. I'd spent just over a month in total in Belgium and I felt it was time to move on once more to warmer climes. I had just turned 20 years old and already I'd already lived rough in two countries, that's rough!

Chapter 12 – Just Warming Up!

With a combination of British pounds and Belgium francs I had about altogether about £150 in my pocket, I decided I wanted a warmer environment and a city that was frost free. My decision was to use most of my money to buy a one-way rail ticket to a far warmer climate, so I went to the Brussels Central train station and looked for trains departing and where they were travelling to. It did not take me long to find one going to Alicante in Spain. My ticket was soon bought, using up the bulk of my remaining funds, but I had to get out of this cold and unwelcoming city. I believed that my onward adventure would carry on for another day at least. I must confess that, at that moment, my adventure was on a day-by-day basis, I would treat every day as it comes and deal with it.

    The train journey was a long one as I travelled south-west, across Belgium, over the border into northern France, around Paris and then across France and down into southern Spain. It was a journey of nearly 1,250 miles and it took about a couple of days to reach my destination. I enjoyed the travelling, the sounds of the train on the tracks and the sounds of the different dialects and languages. It was a safe, warm environment and I enjoyed the change of pace, scenery and the company of the other travellers, many of whom were more than happy to talk to a stranger and even, on one occasion to share their food with me. It was mesmerising to watch the transition in skin tones and dress as I travelled from north-east to south-west.

I had to change trains a couple of times, but I felt that the train was taking me on the right path. Did I miss home? No, not really to be honest. I had always wanted to explore and travel and this was the train ticket to enable me to achieve it, or so I thought. Although the train from Brussels to Paris had been an express train, from Paris south my connection turned out to be a much slower one that stopped in various locations as it headed through France and into Southern Spain. I didn't mind, I was in no particular hurry to arrive as I had no-one waiting for me and nowhere booked to stay – this was not a package holiday, it was me making things up as I went along – much as I had done through much of my life, reacting to each situation as it came along.

In Paris, I changed to a train that would take me on to the next stage of my journey to Perpignan. Much of this journey was done through the night and I tried to catch as much sleep as I could while the seats around me were empty. I managed to get some sleep as I stretched out on the seat on one side of the compartment. We stopped at Montpelier, really the first time that I had seen the sea. From general conversation, I learned that this coastal city had been the base for a large wine producing area but, at the end of the 19th century, a fungal disease had wiped out the vines and now the city is very much a centre of academic excellence. This I noticed, as many young people, mainly French but with a sprinkling of other Europeans judging by the odd snatch of conversation that I heard as they walked past my compartment, alighted here, obviously returning to university. I was travelling and learning along the way, I felt a bit like a young Michael Palin.

After a short stop, the train continued along the coast to Narbonne, another city with a long history, stretching back over 2,000 years. Again, it had been an important harbour but, due to neglect, this silted up and nowadays, boating is more frequently carried out on the local canals, which I could see as the train moved through the city. Another short stop and another change of residents in my carriage and then it was on to Perpignan, another town famous as a wine producing area and home to the well-known Catalan Dragons rugby team.

This time, I had to change trains in order to get to my next stop – Barcelona. This was another long stretch along the coast to Benicassim. Only a small town, it has a wonderful 6km stretch of six fantastic beaches, while at its back is a mountain range that protects it from the worst of the weather from the west. If I had not already decided on my destination, it looked an intriguing place to stop. The thought of being able to soak up that lovely warm, early spring sunshine after the hard, cold nights in Brussels was mouth-wateringly tempting. Never mind, I thought, it is likely to be even warmer where I am going! From here the train meandered its way along the coast to Valencia before trudging on to Barcelona. Another change of trains took me, finally, after a journey of more than 48 hours into the welcoming arms – or so I thought – of Alicante, my destination, where I arrived late at night with – you've guessed it – nowhere to stay. Fortunately, even at this late hour, it was still pleasantly warm and so I wandered out of the station, carrying my last few possessions, and decided to look for the beach. La Playa was easy to find and was a beautiful beach with lush sand that was still warm to the touch. I found a sheltered spot hidden behind a dune and settled down for the night, again very thankful for the remaining warmth left over from a warm Spring day.

I woke early, disturbed by the early morning sounds of a seaside town waking up to a new day. It was only just 6am but already it was starting to warm up, so I decided to stay there a little bit longer and enjoy the warmth after the cold mornings in Brussels. The sun rose high and bright as there were no clouds to hide behind, it was so warm, and I immediately felt relaxed and in good spirits. However, when I finally got up, I was disappointed to see a notice that, obviously, I had not seen in the dark the previous night. The notices were in both Spanish and English. Apparently, on most Spanish beaches, it is forbidden to sleep or to camp on the beaches overnight, the penalty being a fine of up to €1,500! I must have been lucky as no-one had disturbed me! I was gutted, there goes that opportunity, I thought, what shall I do next?

I was now faced with a choice – did I go and spend what was left in my pocket, just a meagre amount of cash, on some food or did I wait until later? I decided to go for an exploratory walk to see what options were open. This was yet another new chapter in my life. I quickly realised that I not in a country where English was widely understood. I was in a foreign speaking country and I didn't speak a single word of Spanish. In hindsight, I probably should have thought of that, I just presumed wherever you go in the world everyone could speak English. I did not have the appropriate visas and I was in an unknown environment, albeit a warm one; I did not know what I was doing there! I quickly realised that I could be in a lot of trouble again, was I jumping out of the frying pan into the fire?

It was early 1991, I had no job, no friends and no life and I thought what do I do next? I started walking round the streets wondering what to do. I quickly discovered that, down by the sea front, it was quite glitzy and the shops that were offering food and drink were quite expensive, so I started to walk back into the older part of town. Certainly, some of the prices were lower but, if I was going to stay in Alicante for long, I was going to have to find some form of income as my last bit of money in my pocket now, was less notes and more coins!

Seeing a sign to the old town – El Barrio – I felt that I had nothing to lose by taking a walk there. It lies directly under the protection of the Castillo de Santa Barbara, the castle overlooking the town. El Barrio features narrow winding streets around the City Hall and the magnificent San Nicholas Cathedral. These streets are full of historic houses, all brightly coloured and plenty of small plazas where I would later go and sit. The only problem was that there were also plenty of little cafés, bars and restaurants from which drifted the most mouth-watering smells, tempting my palette continuously.

Over the next week or two I walked the streets, the squares, the parks and the harbour, trying to find somewhere that I could call "home" but, all too often, the most suitable places were already taken by the "regulars". Eventually, I discovered a corner of one of the parks where I could settle down without being disturbed, either by other members of the homeless community or by the officials. During the day, while I was either walking about or just sitting in the sunshine, I tried to think of ways of generating some urgently needed cash. As I said earlier, I didn't speak Spanish, I had no visas or work permits and I had no fixed abode. What chance did I have?

From what I could see, there did not seem to be a major problem with homeless people in Alicante. The city is a strange paradox for, in the harbour, there are dozens of huge and very expensive yachts belonging to millionaires, while holidaymakers stroll along the elegant sweep of the promenade. At the same time, tucked away in dark corners there are several homeless people whose only bed is a park bench, a doorway, a pavement or the ground under a hedge or tree.

I understand that, now as in Brussels, there are organisations that have been set up to help these people but, when I was there, there was nothing for us, we simply had to make do with wherever we could find. There was nothing glamourous about the use of a park bench as a bed as a last resort, as it was pointed out to me by one frail looking vagrant, his name was Enrique. He had dark mahogany skin with deep wrinkles. I remember he was well educated and he spoke English quite well. He explained to me why he was sleeping on a cold hard bench. He was from Valencia but his shame at the loss of his job as a painter and decorator, followed by the loss of his home, had driven him away, and his tortuous descent had begun. He had no family to help support him as was the norm in Spanish communities. This had happened to him when he was in his early 60's and he said that he had lost hope and was just waiting to die. He drank from a bottle inside a paper bag and had been living on the streets for several years. We became park buddies and would chat for hours at a time while wasting the day away.

How can it be right that an old man such as Enrique who should be living out a peaceful retirement in a place he could call home, is actually sleeping on a stone bench? No walls to protect him from the chill wind, no place to make a cup of coffee, no sink to wash his face, no pillow to rest his head, no chair, no table, no place to hang his clothes, no door to close. Only a thin blanket and a cold stone bench not much more comfortable than an autopsy table to lie on. His old bones unprotected and so alone. I felt so sorry for him.

One day he asked me why I didn't just use my passport to get a room in a hostel and get money from my family. I had been living rough for a couple of weeks by now, when I could have been living in a cheap or modest hotel. I had my passport which gave me UK citizenship and in those days a passport was valuable currency and gave me a certain status. He said that most hoteliers in the city would accept a passport in lieu of payment and would keep it and return it when you check out. I thought to myself why am I sleeping rough when I could be in a nice comfortable room? I thought it was time to check in! That very same day I scouted a few nice but cheap hostels and found a local 2-star hotel that took my passport and gave me in exchange food and accommodation on credit until I checked out. I felt on cloud nine, I was jubilant for the first time in ages! I had a room and bed to sleep in.

The next morning, I sat in the outside patio courtyard of the hostel, with the warm sun on my back and shoulders. I wondered what to do next. What's my next move? What options do I have? I decided to have a walk to try and locate Enrique, to have a chat with him, he might be able to give me some advice. It was around the March time of 1991 I remember the newspaper headlines were saddened by the sudden death of Connor Clapton the son of the musician legend Eric Clapton, Connor was aged just 5 years old had fallen from the 53rd floor, such terribly sad news. I was aged just 21 and I felt such a sharp pain and deep sorrow for a young boy I didn't even know.

However, I had to focus, once again I had no job, no friends, no money, no future. It seemed to be a recurring feature of my life, beginning in England, continuing in Belgium and now starting again in Spain. I was unable to locate Enrique, so I sat on the warm sand by the sea and watched the waves, behind me was the main Alicante High Street with all the shops, restaurants and the commercial sector. As I sat there, the warm breeze from the sea fanned me gently. I was trying to get myself out of my current financial predicament, I noticed all the busy banks and a seed of an idea began. I just sat for ages, thinking and wondering if my idea had any merit. It was a cheeky notion but I wondered if it would work.

    I parked the idea for the time being in the back of my brain and I started trying to think like an entrepreneur – admittedly one with very little money, no work permits, no real residential address and no status - how could I be taken seriously, but, as in the past, I was not afraid to chance my luck. I knew that some millionaires started from scratch without a penny and worked hard to get somewhere, why couldn't I do the same thing? I thought again about my idea for the drop-off boxes that had not worked in Brussels and thought, let's chance my arm and see if I can persuade a bank to let me open an account. I had no collateral, no money and no funding but, what the heck!

Chapter 13 – Cheque Mate

The next afternoon, having cleaned and tidied myself up as best I could, I went into a local bank and said that I had this business idea and I would like to open an account. At the time, the system was a lot simpler than it is now with all the threats of money laundering. I didn't have to deposit funds thankfully to open an account.

The bank simply asked for proof of residency of where I was living – obviously you have to fill in certain forms – and, as I sat there explaining to the man in the bank, he asked for my address and, fortunately, I remembered the hostel address where I had been stopping. The account manager did not seem to take that much heed of the address, and said, "OK if you have got a residency, we will put that down."

I remember waiting about three or four days when, to my surprise, a cheque book arrived at the hostel – I had gone in each day and asked if anything had arrived for me and, one day, they said, "Yes we have this post for you." It was my cheque book.

I felt like celebrating – was my luck finally changing? I had now got a cheque book for an account with no funds in it and I thought what can I use this cheque book for? And then I decided, well, if I can open one account, why don't I open another one? I went to a different bank and opened another account using the same information and, to my amazement, about three or four days later, I received a second cheque book, again for an account with no funds in!

I did it three times in all, ending up with three different cheque books from three different banks, all with my name on them.

Then I thought, what can I do with these cheque books? Having given the matter some serious thought, I wrote three different cheques to three different bank accounts – in those days it was in pesetas, so I wrote three cheques for 100,000 pesetas just to test the water – one cheque into one branch, the second cheque into another branch and the third one into the third branch, just to see whether any of them cleared, which was a dumb idea but it seemed a good idea at the time and I had nothing else to do.

I wanted to go and find Enrique to let him know I had found a hostel and things were looking optimistic. I went to the same park he normally occupied. I was saddened to learn he had been taken into hospital with suspected pneumonia. I feared the worst but hoped for the best. After waiting a few days, I went into one of the banks' branches and asked if the cheque had cleared. I could not believe my ears when I was advised "Yes, the funds cleared into my account this morning."

I said, "Really?"

"Yes, would you like to make a withdrawal?" she asked.

"Well, err, yes I will withdraw the full amount please." I quickly replied.

She promptly handed me the cash in pesetas, and I thought "Wow! I'm rich! I'm on to something here, this is great, what can I do with this?"

I thought well, if this has worked in this branch, maybe it will work in the other branches. I'd now got about the equivalent of five hundred pounds in my pocket - that was a lot of money in those days - and I thought, what shall I do now? So, I decided to chance my luck and I went to the next branch that I had on my list where, unbeknown to me, they seemed from the outset a bit more switched on than the first one. They checked over my withdrawal request with scepticism and then I was asked to wait on a couch in the lounge area.

If I had had my wits about me, I should have walked out quickly, as this was not how it happened at the previous bank. I don't know to this day how they knew that something was wrong and that I was trying to draw funds out of a bank account that had no money in it but, the next thing I remember, was being held down by one of the security guards and taken to the back of the branch where they quite quickly pointed out that I was trying to fraudulently withdraw money that I did not have. I then realised that, if I had just kept the one lot of money from the first bank and walked away, I would probably have been OK, but I just tried to chance my luck once too often.

I was taken into custody by the police, I was read my rights and charged then put in remand until I went before a judge. Everything was conducted in Spanish and I did not understand a word of it – there had obviously been communication between the bank staff and the police.

I was actually in the newspapers - someone showed me a paper, I can't remember the exact headlines, but it went something along the lines of, "Foreigner has a lot of cheek!" I was a nobody trying to manipulate the Spanish banking system! I was sentenced to three months in Fontcalent maximum security prison. I could not believe that I was going to prison for such a petty crime, I honestly thought I'd get a suspended sentence or just deported! They slapped me hard for my cheek and I never did get my passport back!

Going to prison, and to make it worse, in one outside of the UK, I was extremely scared, I was panicking as to what was life going to be like, how was I going to cope, what challenges was I going to face? I was so emotional about the whole idea of being in prison – I just did not know what to do but going to prison was something for which I had not planned, and the outcome was totally out of my hands. I was under the custodial jurisdiction of the Spanish courts and I could not do anything about it. I had no lawyer, no-one was representing me, I just had to face my punishment and do my time.

There were four Modulo's in Fontcalent Prison – it was a high security facility, a behemoth of a prison, close to Alicante, it housed nearly 750 inhabitants with machine-gun carrying guards on each tower, two massive concentric concrete high walls with a further perimeter of razor-sharp electrical wire fencing with guard dog patrols. Modulo One was for the females, Modulo Two was for terrorists, murderers and people involved in gang crimes – quite severe sentences for people who had done some seriously bad stuff – Modulo Three, which was the one that I was placed in, was for misdemeanours, white collar fraud, drug related and minor crimes, and Modulo Four was for the psychologically insane and for those deemed not fit to be safe in any other module, for their own safety, due to the nature of their crime, rapists and paedophiles etc. This prison was built in a desert just outside Alicante about 5 miles away from the city, in the south of Spain.

I entered prison life with considerable trepidation. It was very daunting because I did not know what to expect. Basically, I was crapping myself. You wore the same clothes that you came in – they did not give you any prison uniform. I didn't even have a decent pair of shoes – I was just in flip-flops at the time. In the Modulo that I was in there were only two other English guys and I was put in the same cell as them; you stick with your own. My cell was small and cramped with the three bunk beds taking up the majority of the cell. I was the newbie and all eyes were on me.

My two English cell buddies introduced themselves to me and before I could even put my toiletries down, they both asked eagerly,

"Have you any drugs or money so we can buy drugs?"

I told them I had nothing but the clothes on my back. Both of them had been sentenced for drug related crimes. They seemed nice enough guys. I was tired after being in the administration section and being processed for the last forty-eight hours and said I wanted to just lie down and rest. I was told my bunk was the top bunk which was the worst bunk in the cell - as heat rises it was the warmest part of the cell.

That first night was the worst, the worst by far. The only ventilation was a small barred window which did nothing to alleviate the temperature in the cell. It was so humid the heat could cause a camel to faint. The smell from the open toilet which was only a few feet away was eyewatering. I also had the constant buzzing in my ears from the mosquitoes and finally to make things even worse there was the intermittent clicking noises made by the cockroaches inside the walls and scurrying along the floor; they were driving me insane and this was just the first night. I couldn't sleep a wink. I thought I was in a living hell. I soon realised why the two guys needed drugs!

After a couple of days of settling in to prison life I soon realised that the day-to-day life was extremely regimented and very scheduled. The guards would knock the door loudly with their batons to get you up, do a head count at 5.30am and then you had 10 minutes to make your bunks and mop the floor before you could be allowed outside your cell. Then we had to be down for breakfast at 6.00am. Breakfast normally consisted of yesterday's stale bread and a yoghurt pot with some lukewarm coffee. I used to scoff as many bread rolls as I could in the allocated thirty-minutes I had to eat breakfast. That's why to this day I eat extremely quickly and get a lot of indigestion. I can't help myself.

After breakfast, everyone was made to vacate the prison cafeteria and we then went to the large outside courtyard, walking around until they called us in for lunch, which was normally a soup or warm broth of some kind with a milk carton and back to our cells until we were head counted again and called down for evening meals, which normally consisted of a basic rice and pepper dish or stew with bread.

There was no special protection. It was difficult because you had to be on your toes all the time as you were the new guy. If prisoners weren't chewing bags of sunflower seeds and spitting out the kernels or smoking rollups, they were probably looking to try score a fix. It was a real cauldron of messed up people, and sometimes it was the pure monotony of the situation that sent your mind to seek out another high. There were a lot of drugs being passed around secretly away from the watchful eye of the guards, or in your cell, drugs were weighted at the end of a length of blanket and swung from one prison cell to another. I started taking drugs such as weed or hashish purely out of boredom but mostly to help me get a good night's sleep.

I was always wary of being in areas where I did not recognise anyone, I was the youngster and I always tried to stay with the people that I knew. I would try to find some shade and then sit with my back to the wall so that I could see everything that was happening, and no-one could sneak up on me from behind. In fact, no-one ever did try anything while I was inside. Even though I was only in for a relatively short amount of time I quickly built up certain bonds with other prisoners. Bonding with other prisoners was my rudimentary way of getting protection.

I was always very nervous being inside, you never knew what was going to happen next; you could get to the dinner table and it could all kick off. I was eating paella at the dinner table once when suddenly another prisoner just went up to another, punched him in the side of his face and spat straight into his dinner, I thought this is surreal. I just kept my head down and carried on eating and because the other prisoner didn't fight back his life became hell. The guards never really got involved in individual fights, they weren't paid to be boxing referees. You were there, you could do nothing about it and you just had to ignore it and do your time. I was fortunate because I was only doing 3 months, but, at that time, there were people in there who were doing years for trafficking drugs, taking drugs over the border or dealing in ecstasy at parties and raves.

My crime was more like a misdemeanour. My fellow prisoners didn't look down on me, they would just ask what I was in for, because people were in for so many different crimes. They knew you weren't a total nonce, because they had put you in the appropriate Modulo – they knew it wasn't a major crime but you would still say what you had done – there wasn't a hierarchy or anything – they would just look at you and say, "Oh you are just doing 3 months, you will be out in no time!"

It wasn't just that I wanted to be accepted for what I had done, they just did not think much of it that was all. I suppose that they felt that they couldn't build up that close a friendship with me because I was going to be out in a short time. The other two Englishmen in my cell were in for drugs, one was in for selling drugs while he was at a rave and was caught with some drugs on him, while the other one was done for taking a large quantity of ketamine and MDMA, better known as ecstasy tablets across the border. I remember he got quite a long sentence, something like ten years.

Our cell was about 8ft by 6ft, with the three tier bunks and a separate bricked off smaller area with a wash hand basin and one of those squat-down toilets – a large hole in the floor. The two other guys in my cell were nice guys to be fair, I liked them. Jason was your typical London lad, he liked the sound of his own voice but there was never a dull moment and he used to manufacture ecstasy tablets for his own raves that he organised, but was caught when he tried to take a large quantity across the border.

The other guy, Jamie, was a really nice chilled out guy who used to try to get people into the raves and obviously he would try and sell them ecstasy and whatever other drugs he had on him to feed his lifestyle. Jamie was a really friendly and charismatic guy which I suppose helped in his line of work. Neither of them was hardened criminal types, they were just in the wrong place at the wrong time or like Jason, trying to turn his ability to manufacture drugs and sell them at his raves and make himself a millionaire! – both were probably in their early twenty's, so a bit older than me.

It was difficult for me as I knew that I was in an environment that wasn't 100% safe, but you just played with the cards that you had been dealt. There was a lot going on – a lot of drugs with people getting high all the time with nothing else to do. There was work that you could do – if you were there long enough, you could get assigned a work routine where you could go into the cafeteria or the kitchens, there was a gym where you could go and help out. If you wanted to do stuff, you could earn small wages, but I wasn't in there long enough to be assigned a job and I had no money coming in because nobody knew I was there. I was in there and it was hot. A real contrast with what I had been enduring on the streets of London and Brussels.

Basically, each day was a routine where you knew that you had to be up for a certain time; when they checked the cell in the morning, you had to raise an arm or a head in your cell to be counted. Then after lunch there was the couple of hours siesta period, when you had to go back to the cell and then up again, head count and out for the evening meal. It was lock down round about 7.30pm and that was it until 5.30am the next morning. I remember the day usually involved a lot of constant head counting to make sure the total inmates remained correct and no one had escaped.

The guards were basically OK – there was one we used to call 'Barba' because he had a full-on beard and wasn't the nicest one, he was a real dick! He walked around as if he ruled the place and was quick to dish out a violation if you crossed him. The other guards, in all fairness, were alright with you and simply dealt with you as just another head count, if you didn't fall out of line but, if you caused trouble, they would give you trouble back. In general, prison life was monotonous and boring because it was so regimental – the same process repeated 365 days of the year. However, if you kept your nose clean and didn't piss anyone off, the guards and other inmates generally left you alone and in peace.

Chapter 14 – Gunning for Trouble!

It had been a difficult time in Fontcalent. I came out of prison in just under three months, thinking that that was an experience I will never forget and never want to repeat. However, every now and then life has a way of throwing you a curve ball. Life in prison had a profound effect on my mentality and wellbeing. it did influence me massively, but for all the wrong reasons. I came out of there thinking, 'Well, If I can do that, anything else is going to be a piece of cake?' The other inmates hadn't thought much of my crime and sometimes laughed that I was a lightweight criminal and this did grate on me slightly. I genuinely had a small gnawing part in the back of my head that kept telling me to ignore their childish ridicule but it niggled me, which I know sounds foolish and immature but that was my mentality at that time. I would show them, I thought!

Having come out of jail, I knew that I had two choices, I could either pick myself up or I could sink even lower down and unfortunately, I made the wrong choice and sank further down. I was living rough again in the same place, which did me no favours. Obviously, I just did not know what to do. I was wandering around, in and out of Alicante and, between my time in prison and from wandering the streets, I had picked up a few words of Spanish and was asking for jobs. However, there was no way that I could get a job as I didn't speak the lingo fluently and I had no money. My prison record didn't stop me getting a job, it was simply my inability to speak Spanish that was the major barrier.

I would not tell people where I had been for the last three months, I simply said that I had just arrived. No-one bothered to check – it was before the time of the Internet, so people couldn't carry out a lot of logistical checks on you, you just gave them the information that they wanted to hear and you would either be accepted or not, as the case may be. I was back to square one again and this seemed to be a common theme in my earlier years – up and down, back to square one and so it went on. At the age of just over 21, I had already served three months in prison and my life was going nowhere. I was basically at another low point in my life. I had no friends at all – most of my friends and people I knew were over 2000 miles away.

I was lost, I didn't know what to do next. However, after about a week of living rough as I had no passport to use, I was walking around the streets of Alicante, going into shops, minding my own business and killing time, thinking, 'what can I do, what can I do?' That was when I saw a replica toy gun in one of the store windows. When I first laid eyes on the gun, I knew instinctively it looked like the real McCoy. It was silver and had a realistic look about it, albeit the tip of the gun was painted red. Ok, I know it was a toy replica, but it looked like a decent looking model and the grain of an idea came to me as to what I could do with the it. I thought that maybe I could make some money with it and, as daft as it might sound, I thought well, if I have got a gun, maybe I could rob a bank! If I got away with it then I'd have a load of cash to continue my adventure and if I got caught then at least I'd have a few more bragging rights in prison, that was how my mind whirred at the time!

I was in a Spanish department store called Galletta and I was desperate. I had no money, no work, no friends and I was living rough. Not that living rough was so hard. Living in Spain, even living rough can be ok when you have the beach as your bed and the tide your early morning wake up call, providing that you are not caught, as it is illegal.

Now, I had already been living rough for a week or so after leaving Fontcalent and I was so very, very hungry. Everywhere and everyone around me seemed oblivious to my situation or just preferred to ignore me as their normality continued. It was early morning and people were walking to work, talking to their friends or just sitting and drinking a cortado or an espresso at the local café. I must have stood out like a sore thumb, a young foreign guy with poor quality clothes and unkempt hair and a patchy wayward growth of facial hair. I had tried to obtain work but, only knowing a few Spanish words, it was never going to be easy to obtain a job, plus I did not have the correct work permits or visas. I was alone and scared. I was desperate to just be normal, to have a normal job and a normal life but I was in an unknown foreign environment and was worried that my presence was going to be made known to the authorities and I felt I needed to do this thing sooner rather than later. I had been trying for days to work out how to earn or get money. When you are desperate your mind will try and resolve your situation with desperate and even crazy solutions.

Now, being quite immature and thinking that robbing a bank, using this stolen replica gun sounded like a good idea, my subconscious was feeding these crazy thoughts, like 'Why not?' or 'What have you got to lose?' or 'Just think of the financial gains' and 'No one is going to get hurt with a fake gun.' That was my thought process, get in, get out then seek out a hot shower, a nice dinner, a decent room with a comfy bed and a good night's rest in a cheap hostel or hotel maybe. Well that was the plan. What could go wrong? At this stage in my life, I didn't fully understand the bigger picture or the consequences of my actions.

Without stopping to really think it through and to develop a plan of action – that, after all was not my style! - I went back the next day to the Galleta store, I remember thinking once you start on this path, stick to it. It was hot and I was sweating and my heart was beating faster in my chest however I was in a hopeless situation and needed to get in and out as fast as possible without the security staff or Guardia getting to me first. I was young and naïve but had a massive dose of impulsiveness and a hungry belly to boot. As the adrenalin kicked in, I walked into the store, picked up the gun in its cardboard holder off the shelf and walked straight back out, 15 seconds tops. I walked quickly away and soon realised I hadn't been followed by security. I remember finding a safe place and looking at the gun once I had opened the packet. It had everything I needed to make it look like a real gun, apart from a big red painted mark at the end of the barrel, which showed that it was simply a replica. I thought that if I could get rid of this red marking that would make it look more authentic. Obviously, I had no idea what I was doing, but with the gun in my bag, I decided to walk around and see which banks were open and which seemed to have the lowest footfall and would hopefully make it a quiet bank to rob.

I thought the most daunting challenge now lay ahead of me and I felt sick with guilt and worry. What if this all went wrong? What would I say to my parents? I would be a total disgrace to my family. Forget that, I was already a total disgrace for getting myself in this situation already.

Remember I was the Black Sheep anyway! I had come from a decent family and should never be in a situation where robbing a bank was my only option. But once that idea starts growing in your head, it doesn't stop growing, like a tumour it consumed me. None of my family knew where I was anyway, I hadn't spoken to anyone since I walked out nearly a year before.

I kept thinking I've already been to prison and I know exactly what prison is like; what's the worst that can happen - I'll get caught and get thrown back in the same nick but, on the plus side, I might end up with quite a lot of money and money meant my adventure could continue to who knows where. I knew that I was lonely, having spent the best part of a year on my own, with no friends, nowhere to live, basically working down in London, roughing it while living abroad in Belgium and Spain and now, I wanted to get some familiarity back into my life. This is when this thought process kicked in "I can't get a job, so rob a bank!" It was a constant mantra I kept repeating over and over. I was going crazy.

Basically, there was no real planning involved, it was just a question of walking around Alicante to find the right bank. Obviously, it would not be sensible to pick a big branch in the city centre, I would have to look around the back streets and find a small, local branch. In those days, the banks did not have the full glass counter units. Today, when you walk into a bank, you are faced with big screens with bullet-proof glass, but, in those days, it was simply an open counter as the banks were not as security minded as they are now. Bear in mind, that I am talking about the situation as it was more than 25 years ago. I was fortunate as I happened to find one bank that looked a little bit off the beaten track, it didn't have a lot of people walking past and it wasn't going to create a lot of activity.

I didn't see any security guards on the door, and it looked like a quiet bank with an open counter. There was a small quiet café just down the street, on the other side of the road, so I was able to have a coffee, with some of my last remaining pesetas, and sit in the sun, trying to look relaxed and disinterested in what was going on around me. Little did they know that, inside, my heart was pounding at the thought of what I was planning to do! As the adrenalin and motivation to undertake the most daunting challenge ahead of me rose, I felt sick with guilt and worry. What if this all went wrong? Obviously, I knew the risks involved and I decided that the risks outweighed the losses. I thought that if I could get away with this then, potentially, I've got the money to make decisions on how my life path could continue. I couldn't stand the thought of another night sleeping rough. If I didn't do it today, I might bottle the idea and not go ahead with it. So, I had found a suitable bank and was going to check it out and just go with the flow.

Thus, as I sat there with the last dregs of my coffee, I decided it was simply a case of do or die or what do I do next? I remembered that the gun still had the red marking on it and, that, if anyone saw me pointing the gun with that on it, they would know that it was only a toy and I would be chased out of the bank. I realised that I couldn't do it while sitting outside the café and that I would not only have to go somewhere quiet, but I would also have to find something with which to scratch off the paint.

I finished my coffee, looked up and down the street. I still had not seen anyone going into or coming out of the bank so, obviously, it was not heavily used. I sat there for probably another half an hour and then I saw the bank doors closing – of course, it was siesta time – that would give me time to go and try to remove the paint. Then, while I was sitting there, the waiter came out and set all of the tables up for lunch and there, I was delighted to see, was a knife in each of the paper napkins – just the job and so, while I thought no-one was looking, I took one of the knives and slipped it into my pocket while remaining at the table. Eventually, I decided it was time to go and so I got up and walked casually down the street, away from the café and the bank, but I would be back.

When I left the café. I went to one of the parks that I had come to know, sat on a bench in one of the quieter parts, where I had occasionally slept, took out the gun and the knife and, when I thought that no-one was around, I worked to scrape off the red paint. After a while, using the blunt knife that I had taken from the café, I had removed most of it that would be seen, at least, and sat and rested for a while in the warm winter sun. I tried not to think about what I was planning to do for I felt that if I thought about it too much, I might lose my nerve.

After a while, when more people started to emerge after their siesta, I wandered slowly down to the street where the bank was. I walked past it a few times checking it out, trying not to raise anyone's suspicions, as I built up my courage. My heart was beating out of my chest and I'm thinking 'what am I doing, what am I doing?' But, I thought, if I don't do it now, I am never going to do it. The time is right, there is no-one about, do it! So, I plucked up my courage and I remember walking in casually without trying to make a big deal of it, walked up to the counter, where a very attractive young lady sat at the cash desk. I felt fortunate to see that there were no other customers in the branch as it had only just reopened and the bank staff were casually chatting away. This was not going to be a normal day for anyone. I remember walking in, raising the gun, pointing it at her and asking her to give me the money or, in Spanish *"Dame tu dinero, ahora!"* (Give me your money, now!)

My voice was clear and concise, and I pointed the gun I had stolen only a few hours earlier directly at the nervous female bank teller, who looked in utter shock and I could see the colour drain from her complexion. There were three or four other staff, mostly women, at their desks. It was obvious that they did not know what to do, probably never having been faced with this problem before, they simply sat and looked back at me. There was complete silence. No one moved. I was wondering why things were not happening faster, but either time had just stopped still or everyone was just in shock. The cashier was now observing my fake gun, looking at the end of the false barrel. Her eyes were looking hypnotically at the end of the barrel of my gun, wherever I pointed it she looked at it more and quizzically. I pointed it down, she looked down, I pointed it up, she looked up. Had I scratched off enough of the red paint? I was sweating profusely now and, not having robbed a bank before, I was not sure what to do next. I was in a foreign country, holding up a bank with a fake gun, waiting for the teller to pass me a load of cash.

With no response from her or anyone else for that matter, the seconds were passing and every second was precious, I didn't know whether they were pressing the alarm, and I didn't want to be caught. As I stood there, I suddenly realised that I hadn't checked out whether they had any on-site security - were security personnel suddenly going to rush out and grab me? Nothing happened, nothing at all, she had just frozen on the spot, then after a further few seconds my auto-pilot kicked in. I decided to take matters into my hand, I hopped over the counter (in those days there were no bullet proof glass partitions, well not in this bank) and pointed my gun at the main till with hopefully the cash inside. I was hoping beyond hope there was going to be a lot of money in there. Please let there be money in there. The teller moved slowly towards the till and opened it and I saw a load of notes. I immediately grabbed all the notes in each of the till compartments, while keeping an eye on the handful of employees staring at me and put all the notes into my plastic bag which I had remembered to put in my grungy jean's pockets. With the money safely away, I slid back over the counter and shouted out *"Gracias"* then ran out the door of the bank and ran up a side street as fast as I could. I had been in the bank no more than two minutes but it felt longer.

I'd done it, I'd robbed a frigging bank and I had gotten away, no one got physically hurt and no police involved, it was a clean job. My plan hadn't involved much about what to do or where to go after the robbery. I just ran and ran around the side streets to avoid anyone stopping me – I wanted to get hidden as soon as possible – I ran as far as I could and as quickly as I could, I was young, I was fit, I had speed on my side – through living rough and with my time in jail, I had lost all of puppy fat. Suddenly, I realised that I was drawing attention to myself by running and so I slowed down to a walk, going past some small kiosks and tobacconists. People had been turning around and looking at me but now that I was walking, they quickly lost interest and carried on with their chatting. I remember stopping after about 10 minutes, sweat dripping down my face, stopping to think about what I had done. I looked in the bag, and there was the money and there was the gun. I thought to myself 'You have just robbed a frigging bank!'

I had not been caught but I realised I was still not out of the woods. I was a foreigner and my appearance meant I stood out from the crowd. Obviously, the bank staff would confirm to the police that I was not a Spanish local. Then the realisation of what I had just done came to mind – I hadn't planned this robbery weeks in advance, I had only thought about doing it the previous day and only finalised my decision this morning and there we go! I've robbed a bank and was now holding goodness knows how many thousands of pesetas – I don't how many thousands. I thought "You've done it! Now what do I do next? I had no exit strategy and I didn't know what I was going to do. I was there. I was in Spain. I had all this money and hadn't thought about what to do or where to go. It was as if I was never going to rob it and get to this stage! But I had got to this stage and there I was, but I had no idea as to what to do next.

My first mistake. I should just have got into the nearest taxi and got as far away from where I was as possible. But hindsight is a cruel master and that would have been the clever process and, as I said, I was naïve, definitely no criminal mastermind – I was there, and I was just thinking 'what do I do next'. All I could think of was trying to get myself a nice meal – I hadn't eaten properly for days, as I had been sleeping rough and all I could think of was to find a nice warm hostel or hotel, get myself a warm bath or shower and a nice warm meal. That was my priority and foolish as it might have sounded, after about half an hour, that was what I did. I went and found myself a back-street hostel – it was a bargain basement, one-star if that, but it did the job. I calmed down sufficiently not to bring any unwanted attention from the hotelier or the staff. I walked in and asked in as normal a way as possible for a room for the night. I paid in cash and went up to my room, which was basic but clean. I had thought that I was quite far away from the bank as I had run and run and run but, in the event, I was probably no more than 2km away.

When I was in the room, I decided that now seemed like a good time to throw all the cash on to the bed and swim in it. I had always dreamt of swimming in money, so this felt amazing. I was on cloud nine. I had a long refreshing bath and cleaned up to make myself feel human again. I felt hidden, tucked away in this little nook hole of a hotel in the back streets of the town. I decided after an hour or so, it was time to eat some food. I was starving and salivating at the prospect of a hot meal and maybe a glass of vino. So, I went downstairs to check out what food and drinks were available.

When I went down to the small restaurant to the right of the bar area, there were a few locals sitting at the bar talking, with a lot of arm waving, a lot of gesticulating with a good measure of vocal chin wagging. In amongst the conversation, as I said before my knowledge of Spanish was quite basic, but my ears pricked at the unmistakeable mention of "Banco robado!!" I was on the radar as they must have had a description, I half expected an e-fit of me to appear on the wall-mounted television.

I was startled and I felt like a post-operation patient whose pain killers had worn off. I became extremely nervous and drank the last of my wine and left the remainder of my meal to go back up to the room to quickly put all the money back in the bag and to get out of the hotel as quickly as I could. My worry was my foreign appearance, basically the opposite of what anyone would describe as Spanish. I was a foreigner, a foreign looking person in a foreign country. By now, they must have an e-fit, must know what to look out for, so I must have stuck out like a sore thumb – a lot of the locals were black-haired and I was the exact opposite of what the locals looked like, so this put me even more into panic mode. I thought what shall I do, what shall I do? – I know, I'll just go upstairs, pack up and make a run for it!

This was my Achilles heel and I was scared. I stood out from the crowd but for all the wrong reasons. I left the hotel quickly and walked, I didn't run, as I was trying to be careful not to attract attention. Why didn't I ask the hotel to call me a taxi or simply lie low till the heat had died down a little? However, I was afraid that the hotelier would call the police and let them know about me stopping at his hotel. I was high on paranoia. I tried to leave at the absolute worst possible time. This was my second mistake…

I had only walked a short distance, no more than about 100 metres, when I observed a police car drive past me. My heart was in my mouth and I felt like running, but I continued walking and acting casually. I heard the police car slow to crawling speed and then stop and I heard the police car door open, I instinctively knew the game was up and they were aware of me. I was scared so I ran, and one police officer gave chase while the second got back in the car and tried to keep track of the first, while in hot pursuit of me and his colleague.

I ran like a man possessed along narrow streets and around sharp bends, I ran around people minding their own business, it would have looked comical had it not been for the fact I was the one being chased. The police officer behind kept shouting *"Pare, Pare!"* (meaning Stop, Stop!). All I kept shouting to any passer-by who witnessed the commotion was *"No problema,"* (no problem)! I didn't look behind me as I was trying to avoid capture but I could have been shot at as they did not know whether I was armed and dangerous having just robbed a bank with a gun.

It was only when a local person, who could see the ensuing chase, extended his foot as I ran past him and tripped me up, that I ended up flat on my face with the plastic bag spewing out loads of peseta notes all over the narrow street. The chase was over and, no doubt, the local man still dines out on the day he stopped a bank robber in his tracks with his right leg, who knows?

My only saving grace was that when I was caught and the police handcuffed me and collected my plastic bag, the bag not only contained the hundreds of thousands of pesetas but also the plastic gun which I had used to rob the bank. This piece of evidence was used in my trial.

Chapter 15 – Banged to Rights!

After my second capture, I was held for incarceration in an Administration Cell in Fontcalent, the same prison as before, and where I was held until I was processed by the Administration Department. I remember thinking "I hope I get back into Modulo 3!" which I had only left about two or three weeks before, as at least I know a couple of people already in there! This was my thought process, but I was concerned that it might mean that, this time, I would be deemed to be of a higher risk than the type of offence that I had committed previously and maybe I might end up in a different Modulo. As I explained upon my first incarceration, different Modulo's had different types of offenders and different regimes, so that was my main concern.

I was quite tubby when I was younger and my baby fat had stuck around for far too long, so I thought that, if nothing else, maybe this experience is going to make me a lot thinner! I must confess to having lost some weight during my first stay and through my time sleeping rough for all those months, but, obviously, I had to believe that I would be looking at a longer stay on this occasion. I still tried to think out all the positives that I could, even in bad situations and, even while I was held in the Administration Cell,

Why was I in prison for a second time? Was it because I wanted to be anywhere but home or was it because I enjoyed being punished? My life was totally off the rails by the time I was still only 21 years old. I think I needed the time in prison for reflection and basically to try and discover the person I was, incarceration started with remand so I was kept in solitary confinement and was left alone for 99% of the time while I was being processed and for due diligence to be done as to which Modulo I was to go into and also which cell.

The time spent waiting in solitary confinement while on remand played with my mind, I was just waiting for the inevitable call to be transferred and not knowing my ultimate destination heightened my fear and pumped up my adrenalin a few notches. Would I end up in a junkie's cell who was nuts or a psycho's cell who would just batter me for being foreign. Or Modulo 2 which had all the gangs and murderers. All these thoughts constantly went through my mind. Which Modulo would I get?

I was monitored constantly until I was moved into the main prison. I was being assessed to ensure that I would be going into the correct section. I had to maintain my spirits so, once I was going back and indoctrinated back into prison life, I remember before, I found books a big consolation and I used to live with a book to read. I lost so much weight and felt so emaciated by a lack of nourishment as I was living on the food rations, since I could not afford any of the extra food that could be purchased from the prison kiosk. Permission was required in order to do everything, from going to the toilet to taking a shower; it made me feel that I was being brainwashed, as the pressure makes you become more and more sub-human and almost akin to a robot.

Once, while I was in solitary confinement, awaiting processing, I kept shouting and repeating over and over again to an Administrator my request for "Modulo 3!" but, in hindsight, this could have backfired because they might have thought that I was trying to manipulate the system in some way or going crazy and could end up in Modulo 4. However, my young appearance must have convinced anyone who cared that I was no serious threat to them. I kept speaking in Spanish *"Secunda vez, mis amigos son in Modulo tres!"* that this was my second time and that I wanted to see my friends in Modulo 3! Apparently, this repeated mantra worked and when I was finally admitted back into prison life, I was put back into Modulo 3, which was a massive relief!

As soon as I was transferred, it was back to the small and grimy cells, with their three bunk beds, their grimy wash basin with its single tap which emitted warm discoloured water and, worst of all, the disgusting open hole to squat over to do your business. It was such a crowded environment with a total lack of privacy. Cut off from society, it was a totally different lifestyle to anything you could ever imagine. I know I was expecting punishment but to end up in a cell where your cell mate would suddenly urinate out of the window was not something I easily got used to.

Some prisoners were crazy and would pace the yard, talking gibberish out loud or just stand wailing, with their arms in the air. I thought this can't be right, surely, they should be put into a different module that can help them. It was a weird and extremely frightening mix of people, hence the reason I never associated myself with many people apart from my own cell mates or a few other English-speaking people.

I remember meeting up with the two English guys that I had seen previously, plus some new ones whom I hadn't met before, and they were shocked to see me again, as you can imagine! They thought that I would have learned my lesson but here I was, back again. I was put back in the same cell I had vacated only a few weeks earlier with Jason and Jamie. There was a new guy there, called Dave, who asked me if I had any dope with me and what I was banged up for. The order apparently was the same in most prisons – drugs first, then general interest in your offence next! There was a certain hierarchy in prison life according to the offence that you had committed, and the sentence attached to it, so doing something for 10-15 years at a stretch is considered on a higher level than a six-month sentence. When I told them that I had just robbed a bank, all their jaws dropped!

"You know you'll get a long stretch for that", they all said! "Probably 10 years!"

This was something that I had not considered, neither had I really thought about how much time I was going to have to do to pay for my crime. The thought of doing 10 years hit me like a stone! Have you ever been lying in bed and you suddenly get a jolt in your body? That sudden realisation. I remember thinking 'Shit - this is my life totally messed up and ruined! I am 21 and totally screwed up. By the time I get out of here, I'm going to be in my thirties!'

That sudden realisation hit me to the core and again showed my immaturity, even at the age I was. I was living in the "now" without any thought of the future and the consequences of my actions. I hadn't lived a life, I hadn't settled down and I hadn't found love, I hadn't had a family life, and all this was now being taken away from me, at least for a considerable number of years. I was stuck in a foreign maximum-security prison trying to impress all the wrong people, people who would all be leaving before me, while I remained stuck in this existence. When you are in a foreign prison, you basically stick with your own nationality and, in that way, there is a certain bond among brothers and I never really got threatened as I was never a loud mouth or a wide boy, I just wanted to fly under the radar.

I was the youngest English prisoner and I suppose that that gave me a slight advantage, no-one saw me as a threat, and I suppose they basically just felt sorry for me. That was apart from a loudmouth called Eddie, from Essex, who was a bit of a wide boy. He used to walk with a swagger and talk out loud. His whole attitude was designed to give the impression that he was not to be messed with. I would keep well away from him as I was slightly intimidated by him. I used to find his attitude quite obnoxious but that was just the way that he was. He never bullied me or shouted at me, but he liked to tell everyone that he had been banged up for beating up a police officer and the distribution of class A drugs. He was everything that I was not – we were like binary numbers.

There was another chap who was also in for drugs, it seemed that everyone who was English was in for drugs – apart from me! His name was Ian. He was a nice lad, a similar age to me, maybe slightly older. We just wanted to get high and to experience everything that life had to offer. I gelled quickly with him as he was a thinker and we would ponder life's questions. He would always be asking questions, like what was outside the universe, how big the universe was and how small we are in comparison. I really liked him and always felt calm when I was around him. When we sat down in the outside courtyard, we always sat with our backs to the wall so that no-one could creep up on us from behind. I was often alone with my thoughts as I had no regular income, unlike most of the other prisoners and, in addition, I did not speak any Spanish so all the plum jobs that were available went to the Spanish prisoners.

I basically did whatever I could to make the days count down more quickly. Initially, I had no money, I was skint so could not rely on my prison bank account, which a lot of inmates used to provide some "niceties", for example, extra food from the tuck shop. The prison authorities didn't give us any money, you simply relied on whatever they provided. My bank robbing money had obviously been confiscated, I had no money, I just had the clothes that I wore – including my flip-flops. I did apply for a position helping out in the gym, it was voluntary so non-paying but I was told my sentence meant I couldn't do the voluntary gym work, which at least would have got me out of the Yard on a daily basis. Every yard day counted as a day inside prison. I was disappointed not to get this cherished opportunity to leave the modulo but I understood.

After about 9 months or so inside, I was finding this lack of money a complete strain. I had yet to be tried or given a court date and no one from the British Consulate made any attempts to visit me. I longed for cash to buy some of the few niceties that were on offer. Everyone else seemed to either have their own bank accounts or were given money on a regular basis by the friends and relatives that visited them, but that was never going to happen to me in my situation. I kept being told by other prisoners to simply ask for help – if you need help simply ask for it or write to a family member and ask them. However, I did not want to put my family to shame over what I had done and where I was now. Rightly or wrongly, I just preferred to do my time.

However, the idea of making money was always in the back of my mind. After a while, I noticed that, when the kiosk closed, many prisoners, particularly the Spanish, craved for more caffeine. I thought that I might be able to facilitate this and, consequently, be able to earn some pesetas that I could take back to my cell to pay my way. Basically, I wanted to bring something back to my cell mates as I had been a bit of a freeloader. They had shared things with me, but I had not been able to give them anything back. They used to bring things into our cell, drugs or things from the kiosk and would share it around, but I was in no position to reciprocate.

I got on well with Alberto who managed the kiosk. He was a small, elderly Spanish gentleman with long grey hair tied back in a ponytail and he always had a smile on his face. His English was a lot better than my Spanish, so I was able to put a business proposition to him. I offered to rent a pump-action thermos from him with the long-term aim of buying it, but I wanted to test out the waters first. I agreed to pay him 100 pesetas a day and that would cover the coffee machine, the coffee and 20 plastic cups. Then I would sell the coffee for 25 pesetas each for a single shot of coffee or 50 pesetas for the stronger, double shot that many craved. It was not long before word had spread that I was the man to go to when the kiosk was closed. I had a long line of Spanish asking for espressos and I had them coming up to me, even during the day when the kiosk was still open, asking if they could pay now for one later, after the kiosk had closed. They absolutely loved their dose of coffee, the stronger the better.

After the first week, I was making 500-1,000 pesetas a day (about £2.50-£5.00 a day). It might not sound a lot but when you consider that the most that you could take out of your bank account in a week was just 10,000 pesetas, then I was not doing too badly at all! I enjoyed having this monopoly on the coffee, but I made sure that Alberto got his rent first thing every day, before he had the chance to ask for it. I didn't want him to have any reason to take this money-making scheme away from me. Although the people with whom I was dealing were baddies, I never came under any pressure from any of the other prisoners. In fact, I believe that I had a bit of an easy ride from them as they felt sorry for me.

Once the kiosk closed, I was open for business. They knew where I was, as I was always in the same spot. I made as much as I could, to be honest. I had no problems from the guards as they were locked behind their double doors and, while they were obviously monitoring the courtyard on their TV screens, they were not bothered about what I was doing. After all, I was not causing any problems. That was my way of contributing to life in our cell, for drugs and any other goodies.

Basically, there were no problems at that time but, one day, one of my cellmates, Jamie came back in the evening and told us one of his Columbian friends had come up to him in the courtyard and said, "Would you like to see this magazine that I have got?" Now you must remember that many of these guys had been banged up for a considerable amount of time and had had no opportunity for sex. The circulation of these magazines was basically all that was on offer.

It was just me and Jamie in the cell at that moment, Jason was probably in the courtyard still, the next thing I remember, Jamie was saying to me was, "Look, if you would like to read this magazine Sean, I will suck you off. You can imagine that I am a woman who is doing this to you!" I was shocked and told him, quite pointedly, to go and suck himself off! It was strange as I had never thought of Jamie as being bisexual and he had never given either of us any impression of those sorts of tendencies. But prison can change people. The magazines were passed around from cell to cell. They would be tied to a piece of rope and lowered out of the cell window where they could be picked up by someone in another cell and thus widely circulated! This was how many inmates got their kicks. Kicks and a Fix was a nightly thing in a lot of cells.

Life in a foreign prison, what was it like? It was just a mundane sequence of events that repeated themselves over and over again, like Groundhog Day but with walls! I was quite familiar with it, as I was in the same cell as when I was locked up a few weeks earlier – the same triple bunk bed, the same wash basin, the same 'squatter' toilet. Again, we were woken up at 5.30am, wave your arm or raise your head to be counted. You never really left your bunk unless you needed to, or you had to use the 'squatter.' Once morning roll call was ended, you tidied up, mopped your cell room floor and left for breakfast. Walking down to breakfast, which was in a large steel cafeteria that accommodated about 250 prisoners at any one time, you found yourself any free space at a table and then checked out what food was on offer.

It's amazing how snobby you are at first about eating stale bread for breakfast but, after a few weeks, that stale bread and yoghurt began to taste normal! Your taste buds are such an underrated part of your body, but they help you survive as they adjust, just like adjusting a TV tuner, around whatever you put in your mouth. It might taste like crap for the first few days but, after a while, your taste buds retune themselves. Soon, I began to enjoy dunking my stale roll into my yoghurt pot - strange but true – it became almost normal!

Once breakfast was over, about 7.30am, we were escorted into the outer courtyard, where each nationality tended to have its own spot or section. The prison courtyard or yard is where you walked and talked and if you had money you did business. Then the hunt for drugs began. Drugs were relatively unknown to me before I entered prison life, apart from my short stay in Brussels, but they soon became part and parcel of my day-to-day existence – hashish, marijuana, pot – there was nothing that couldn't be obtained – there were stronger drugs, but I was not into them. Basically, they were orally ingested or smoked. There were drug addicts who would find a corner that was not visually obvious and inject, for example in the outside toilets. I noticed that, unless you were doing something to draw attention to yourself, then the prison guards would stay behind their own walls. Attract their attention through visibly injecting or by fighting, and they would be down on you like the proverbial ton of bricks!

One day I was moved into another cell, it was a shock but cell swaps happened a lot. I was lucky as it was a two-bunk cell which just meant you had slightly more available room to move around each other. Again, I was in luck, my new cellmate - I will call him Lee - was a tall, well-spoken British guy who had been found by the police with a bag of drugs, he had been grassed up and his lawyer reckoned he would get 4 or 5 years. Lee would talk and he knew how to get drugs on the never-never or even how to just scrounge for them. I used to watch him in action scrounging for drugs, even for just the smallest piece of hash and I thought 'Wow, this guy has really got the gift of the gab and no shame whatsoever!' He didn't give a fuck. He would always come back to our cell at lockdown with a score - I felt like one of those little birds in the nest just waiting patiently for the parent to fly back and regurgitate and it was similar for us with the hash to smoke - he hadn't regurgitated it, but it just reminded me of that scenario!

If we weren't trying to wonder where our next smoke was coming from, we would spend the morning pacing up and down the yard, bearing in mind that this was the south of Spain where the temperature was always quite warm at worst and very hot at other times, particularly at mid-day. In the early morning, I used to walk with people that I knew, as I never felt comfortable on my own. I walked and I walked and just listened to what people had to say – most of it was just bullshit, but it passed the time. I must have walked miles each day as I soon noticed that my clothes were getting looser and baggier. You were not supplied with any prison uniform, just the clothes that you came in with, unless you had any sent to you by your family or friends. I tended to rely on cast-offs or, if someone I knew was leaving prison, I used to just ask them if they had any clothes or toiletries that I could have. That was the hard part of prison, saying goodbye to people – I said a lot of goodbyes while I was there.

Basically, you were out in the yard from immediately after breakfast until they called you in for lunch – you spent a lot more time out of your cell than you did inside, whereas the ETA terrorists who were in one of the other Modulo's, were locked up for 23 hours per day and were only allowed out for one hour per day when we were locked up in our cells, i.e., after about 6.30pm.

At noon, there was a rollcall in the yard, when everyone had to line up and be counted by the prison guards – it was a waiting game mostly. Have they got the numbers, are the numbers correct? The figures then had to be passed up the chain of command until the chief guard was happy that everyone who should be there was there. Once rollcall was over, we could all file into the cafeteria for lunch. We would line up, get our tray and queue for our pigswill broth and potatoes that was half-heartedly ladled upon our plate. By the end of the first month, this pigswill began to taste like normal food! Albeit a basic version of food, it was half edible – some type of meat-based frothy soup, half-cooked, with some milk or water to drink – it was basic. Prison officials must have cornered the market on mini yoghurts, because we had them every day, morning, noon and evening meal! I've never eaten one since!

After lunch, it was back outside for more walking or, if you were lucky, you were invited to a small hiding spot out of the eye line of the tower guards for a quick puff or a quick drag from a bottle containing some hash. As you can imagine, from never having smoked to getting this shit into my body, I very quickly got high. Sometimes, to the discomfort of Lee, I would get a little spaced out and could attract the attention of a guard, so obviously, he was a bit worried as you weren't supposed to do this. If I was looking pasty when we went back to our cell, I would stand out as being stoned – I didn't really care that much - what were they going to do, bang me up? Lee had my back though and would always try and talk to the guards if I was as high a kite so I could walk past them unchallenged.

I used to play a lot of chess back home and I found a chess set in the Library. I would while away the hours until it was time to go back in for dinner playing chess with whoever was available. It probably all sounds rather easy - it was, since Modulo 3 had all the people who were not volatile and not likely to cause trouble at the first sign or mention of fight. We were in the "easy" pod, but the days were extremely tiring, being out in the baking heat, apart from mealtimes with only a single tap for water. Unless you had access to some funds, you were screwed really – you just had to rely on whatever handouts people were prepared to give you while, for drink there was only the outside water taps. Until I started my coffee business, I had never had any money to go to the tuckshop so just had not bothered with it. However, with the profits from the coffee sales coming in, we could afford to get ourselves some drugs and food for our munchies afterwards. I also learnt the skilful game of backgammon and would play that game for a few hours whilst waiting for time to pass by, I became quite good at backgammon.

At this stage, I still had not been to court, I was still waiting.

What I used to look forward to each day was the final rollcall. You were in your cell all evening and left in peace until the next morning. We would have had our evening meal – it was three meals per day. Dinner, again, was quite basic as I remember – something like paella with another stale bread roll, followed by another mini-yoghurt if you wanted one! If we were lucky, Lee would have been on his daily track-a-fix recon mission and, once everyone was banged up and the guards had left us in peace, we could have some dope. We did anything to keep us high and doped up as this at least deafened our hearing and stopped the incessant noise from the creepy night-roaches and the mosquitoes from driving me bat shit crazy. Drugs let me have a half decent night's sleep and stopped me going insane. Lee was the master of either rolling a joint, if we had enough or, if there was only a small amount, he would find a large 1litre water bottle, put some tin foil over the covering and prick a few holes then put the hash on the top, then score a hole near the top with a pen and use the tube from the pen to suck the smoke at the top from the burning hash. I remember the first time I sucked the hash; my body almost froze with the shock of the high and I turned a shade of white and I was then violently sick in the squatter. And then I was probably sick again because I just had my head in the squatter!

I remember, after about ten months, I was told that I was going to be taken for trial. I was taken to be sentenced – I didn't have a lawyer; no-one would waste their time on me as I was a bank robber who had been banged to rights with everything on him. The court case was just a day out for me. I didn't understand a word they said. They were obviously talking in Spanish, the hammer went down, I turned around, and asked, *"what is it"* and some guy said *"Ocho Annos"*. By that time, I had a small amount of Spanish and I said *"What, eight years!?"* and they nodded. I was still shocked to be handed an eight-year sentence, even though I knew it was a serious crime but, as I said, it could have been more. If they had picked up that bag and there had been a real gun in there, it could have been 15 years, as there would have perceived to have been intention to cause serious harm on my part, so it could have been a lot worse. They would have believed that there could have been a real potential loss of life threat. It was a kind of blessing in disguise as they found everything in that bag.

I was grateful for small mercies – eight years, I worked out, was nearly 3,000 days to be incarcerated and, at 21, this felt like a life sentence! All I could think about was if I did half the mandatory eight-year sentence I was going to be doing fifteen hundred yards or days in this prison courtyard! This filled me with utter dread and a gut wrenching sick feeling in the depth of my stomach . I felt numb but I knew that my sentence reflected my crime and

I knew that I had done wrong and deserved punishing, but it still came as a massive 'fuck me!' kind of moment. I was screwed, my life was screwed, and I thought that my life was never going to be the same again.

Even though I was now just 22, I felt that my life was over, I would be washed up and finished when I left Fontcalent and I would have to restart my life completely from scratch. I was screwed! With hindsight, it was going to be one of those moments that I would use repeatedly – my darkest hour so to speak – nothing could get worse than how I felt at that moment. Looking back, it has always been an anchor point that I can reflect on when things seem a bit hopeless. I know that things can't be as bad as being 22 and having an eight-year sentence in a foreign maximum-security prison ahead of you – grim - but nothing can compare with that and being totally isolated – no friend, no life, no contacts, nothing! It was far worse even than the months that I had spent sleeping rough in London and Brussels. At least during those times, I was able to make my own decisions as to what I wanted to do, even if I perceived the options to be limited, they were still considerably more than were available to me in prison.

I didn't tell my family about my situation as I didn't want to cause them undue stress. At that time, I didn't have any way of telling them, but this was to change when I met another 'giddy' – that was what the Spanish called us foreigners – who was banged up for drugs, who said he had been framed. He owned a bar in town, not far away from where I was first caught and, over time, we became friends. On one occasion, I asked him if I could use his bar as a forwarding address, which would avoid my letters arriving taped up with Sellotape. If you just sent a letter straight from Fontcalent Prison, it would have Sellotape along the top where the authorities had opened it to make sure there was nothing in it that there should not have been and it would also have the Fontcalent Modulo Tres stamp on it, so this would be a red flag to anyone who received the letter! In order to avoid suspicion, I asked my friend if I could use his bar, I think it was in the Altea district of Alicante where, if I sent my letters to his bar, they would open them and then forward the letter inside to my family at our home address in Birmingham.

I wanted to get in contact with my family – I didn't want them to worry about me as they hadn't heard from me for more than two years. I hadn't communicated with them or anyone. They did not know where I was and I didn't think me telling them was a good idea, mainly because I was ashamed and embarrassed. I believed that they must have been worried sick and so I thought that, in this way, I could just use his address to say to them that I was working in this bar, I'm having a great time, you don't need to worry about me and I'm ok! He said *"No problem. You send your letters to my bar with your forwarding address and I will make sure they get sent to your family, so avoiding any suspicion."*

In this way, I could get my mail to my family every six months or so to let them know that I was safe and working in a Spanish bar and living life to the max! I used these letters as a way of escaping from the walls that surrounded me and imagining what I would be doing if I was a free agent and living outside the prison. My letters would go on the lines of *"Hi Mom and Dad, I am having a great time, lots of parties, please don't worry about me, I'm just fine, Love, Sean"*

Basically, the idea was to let them know that I was alive. In hindsight, my friend who was in prison with me said to me once "*You know what you should have done Sean, you Muppet, you should have just found an English-speaking bar here in Spain, having already worked in an English pub, you would have found work easily!*"

So, if I had just gone into an English-speaking bar in Spain, I wouldn't have been in my present situation. However, hindsight is a very precise science and as a very naïve 21-year old who was very immature, I stood no chance. That's how naïve and stupid I was! I cannot believe that I did not think of going into an English bar and pulling pints. A real 24-carat dope I was! I was so consumed by my tunnel-vision that I never took another moment to check out my other options. Once I came up with my only plausible plan to rob a god-damned bank, I never deviated. Now I always know there is always at least one other option!

I had taken an eight-year sabbatical in my life instead of using my brain to find a job in an English bar, probably would have found one in 24 hours! What a shocker! Maybe in my immaturity, I had always wanted to get caught, just to go back to the prison, just to show the inmates what I had achieved and to get lavished with some diluted respect, or maybe subconsciously I preferred prison to the idea of going back home– who knows?. I had the chromosomes of an idiot but one thing that I learned and remember to this day, is always to think of my options and always to rule out Option 1 straightaway – there are always other better options than Option 1, if you put your mind to it.

Chapter 16 – Fight or Flight?

I was in prison for several years and, with time, you get to meet a lot of characters. I can't remember most of their names, but there was one person there who I found quite amusing. He was a Columbian guy who had no friends and so was like me and we bonded quite quickly. He was only in there for about 6 months for some misdemeanour, but we got on quite well. He mixed in with the group of English people there as he could speak English very well. He communicated very well on our behalf because, obviously, he could speak Spanish fluently and he acted as our translator.

He would promise us the world – *"When I leave here, I am going to send you books, clothes, I have access to a lot of money and there are people out there that I know who will help me get you guys jobs when you come out, so don't worry as I will be your "go-to" guy."* He left prison after about six months and we said our goodbyes *"hope we never see you again!"* and *"don't forget to communicate"*, we said.

"No, no worry, I'm going to be your main man!" he replied.

We never heard anything from this guy, he never communicated diddley squat. he never sent us a letter, nothing and then about 6 months later, he got caught again and he got sent back to the same Modulo! So, as you can imagine, he got some serious stick.

"Yeah, I am really sorry guys, I'm not a liar, I just had loads to sort out!"-Blah, Blah, Blah!

We saw the amusing side because when you are inside, you can say anything and I can understand, because when I eventually got outside, I said I would communicate and write letters but, once you are outside, your life changes totally and you don't ever communicate or at least, you try not to look back, except to use it as a serious mistake that you promise never to commit again. You have the right intentions but, once outside, you refocus, you reappraise what you are going to do and your life changes completely. You close the door on it – it's a chapter closed. You want to move forwards not look backwards.

There was another guy that came in. He was a London guy, I won't tell you his name as I have seen him on TV since, I'll call him Kieron and he thought that he was some sort of a London wide boy. He had this quite comical wide stance walk and talked loud and brash. He wasn't, bless him – he had all the jewels – you could keep your jewellery while you were inside, if they didn't get taken off and registered in the processing unit - and I remember that he had a gold chain and rings. Obviously before he came in, he must have thought *"I am going to be the hardest guy I can think of!"*. He was trying to blag his way through his sentence and maybe use his gold as currency. That didn't wash well with one particular Italian by the name of Gino who just looked straight through him and said, *"Do you know what, Kieron? You're just a wanker-blagger!"*. Gino snatched the gold chain from around his neck. Snapped it straight off his neck. Do you know what Kieron did, the wide boy from London, he cried! That was probably the sorriest I ever felt for anyone ever inside prison. His cover was blown and he had lost a gold chain. Kieron was as placid as a pussy cat for the rest of his time. A few days after the incident a few of us Giddy's felt sorry for him and asked Gino to hand back his gold chain which, to be fair to him, he did.

When I was in jail the first time, I kept very much to myself or with the two Brits with whom I shared a cell. This time it turned out to be much different. Because I was perceived as being inside for much longer, I got to know and see a lot more of the long-timers – men who were serving anything from ten years and over. These were not the real hardliners – the murderers and rapists – as they were in Modulos 2 and 4. However, some of these were trouble enough. I shared the prison with a wide mix of nationalities ranging from European countries to South America. It became increasingly obvious that the majority of these were in for drug-related crimes – growing, selling or simply possession with the aim of selling. Not only were they a mix of races but also a mix of ages. Just sitting watching, I could see clique groups in their own particular areas of the courtyard, with the older ones dominating the younger ones and getting them running around doing errands for them.

Over the time that I was in that prison, there were numerous fights and a couple of stabbings. Mostly, they were over stolen drugs or money. In the main, each nationality tended to keep together and to stay away from other groups but, men being men and with everyone permanently cooped up for eight hours a day, tensions often did arise. In most cases, however, the sudden appearance of guards banging their batons was enough to quell any problems.

One day, when I was sitting out under one of the shelters in the yard, I heard an argument building up. I didn't understand what they were saying but it soon became apparent that something had gone wrong within one of the South American groups. The next thing that happened was that words turned to fists and one of the younger men, about six feet tall and about 14 stone, lashed out at the older man – probably aged about 60, silver grey hair, only about five feet tall with shoulders as wide as a Sherman tank! The younger man, probably mid-twenties and as brown as a berry, obviously thought that being younger, he would be quicker and could easily defeat the old man.

How wrong he was, for although the older man was slower, he had years more experience of fighting. Not only that but he had probably learned his skills in the back street of a city such as Rio de Janeiro as a member of one of the many street gangs, where fighting does not follow the Marquess of Queensbury rules! Sure enough, within what seemed like seconds, the younger man was being put in a headlock and having his face smashed in, then thrown on the ground, where the older man jumped on him and started pummelling his face and head. Soon, there was blood everywhere where the young guy lay as first his nose and then his mouth was split wide open. The younger guy's brother got involved and soon I saw about ten inmates jumping in and it all kicked off, big time! With all the commotion, it wasn't long before there was a lot of whistle blowing as the guards came rushing out on to the scene. However, by the time that they got there, all the protagonists had disappeared into other groups around the yard, just leaving the bleeding youngster on the ground, needing A&E.

That brought a sudden end to the sojourn in the sunshine for that afternoon, as we were all hurried back to our cells while the guards tried to investigate what had happened –

without any success of course! The following day, we were all put on shortened rations – not that we got much anyway! I subsequently discovered from one of my cellmates that the problem had arisen over drugs – now there's a surprise. Apparently, the younger man had tried to steal some drugs from the older man and had been caught in the act.

As far as I could see, after this event, things went quiet for a while, for two reasons. First everyone was wary about the ramifications of that fight and second, the guards made their presence more obvious throughout the day, in contrast to before the fight, when they would just appear sporadically in ones and twos. However, from the message that went around the jail, it was obvious that the peace and quiet was not going to last.

Sure enough, about two weeks later, there was another outburst. Apparently on this occasion, a large stash of drug money had gone missing and the next thing that happened was a mêlée involving about 30 prisoners, as more and more waded in on both sides. This time, the reaction was swifter and more vicious, as a group of about 15 guards, batons waving, waded into the middle of the fight, not bothering to sort out who was on which side and who was to blame. Their only concern was to stop what they saw as something that could rapidly get out of hand and develop into a much bigger round of trouble. Within minutes, it seemed, there were many prisoners on the ground, with blood streaming from head wounds, prisoners, holding arms that were potentially badly bruised if not actually broken. Half a dozen of them were rounded up by the guards and taken off, presumably to solitary confinement, as we did not see them for a few days.

If you were unlucky enough to be sent to solitary confinement, you were banged up for maybe a week or ten days when you would not see anyone and your food would be handed to you through a slot in the door. New inmates were also put in solitary for about a week when they first came in as, indeed I was. I must confess that that builds up the tension. You know that you are entering an unknown world where all sorts of men were imprisoned, some for many, many years and you just did not know what was going to happen.

It was becoming increasingly obvious to me that while this prison, because of the way that prisoners were segregated, was not one of the worst or most violent, it was certainly no picnic – not that it ever should be. As I said earlier, the population inside Fontcalent was very mixed, comprising mainly Europeans and South Americans. There was also a mix of religions and of ages. Some, as I had been on my first prison stay, were only in for a very short time, while others were facing decades of being locked up. These factors in themselves were enough to generate a deal of tension and at times, it did not take a great deal to spark problems. Different personalities, religions and ethnic origin are a volatile combination and like any chemical reaction can ignite in just the briefest of moments. If you then add into this the fact that we were all banged up in our hot and stinking cells for a large portion of the day, it is not difficult to see how problems could, and did arise.

While friendships did develop, especially within national groups, if you put 250 men per modulo in that type of environment for a long time, then things will inevitably happen. However, on this particular occasion, the severity of the thirty-man brawl and the resultant immediate reaction of the guards seemed to have a quietening effect, for it was many weeks before trouble brewed again. I am not sure what happened but suddenly, all the prisoners were sent back to their cells quite early in the afternoon.

I discovered later that one of the South American prisoners had been seething from a previous altercation and by something that had been said about his parentage. One thing led to another and the next thing was that one of them was lying on the ground in the restaurant with blood pouring out of his side and a knife was lying on the floor beside him. No-one ever discovered from where he had got the knife, maybe the kitchens but he certainly made use of it. We were all held on shutdown, apart from being allowed out for meals, until the guards had sorted out what had happened. Eventually after about three days, life gradually returned to normal, as we were, once again, let out. We were told by other South Americans, that the one who had done the stabbing was the brother of the young guy involved in the previous fight and who had been taken away, while the one who had been stabbed, was the elderly man with the Sherman tank shoulders, who had died.

That, thank goodness, was the worst event that happened while I was in that jail, although there were many, many other smaller outbreaks of violence. Although there was a programme of work that could be attempted and training courses that could be undertaken, the majority of the inmates were not in the least interested in these activities, leading to boredom and creating an atmosphere of tension at times, as we all wondered what might happen next.

There was another occasion that sticks in my mind above all the other minor scuffles. This was about three years into my stretch and, once again, involved the South Americans. I am not sure to this day what exactly started it all, but I do remember that, one very hot and steamy afternoon when everyone's tempers were fraying, there was a huge mêlée in the yard. There seemed to be about 15 or 20 prisoners involved. Suddenly, the atmosphere changed as the sunlight caught once more, on a knife blade – where it had come from, I did not know, but the implications were obvious.

Some of the prisoners started to disperse quite rapidly as they did not want a recurrence of the previous incident, while others started shouting for the guards. It then became obvious that, in fact, more than one blade was in action and the fighting suddenly became limited to a handful of prisoners as the guards appeared and started laying into everyone around with their batons. For a few minutes, it became quite frightening but then, it was all over as the guards grabbed about four of the ringleaders and hauled them away, some of them covered in blood. We did not see the South American ringleaders again as we heard they had been moved into another modulo. It was quite unusual to be moved into another Modulo midway through a sentence. It was noticeable, however, that the Europeans gave the South Americans a wide berth for a while – until of course, they needed access to their seemingly never-ending stream of drugs!

Because I was in for longer on this second occasion, I did eventually get involved with the work programmes. They didn't give out work jobs to those on short sentences – they wanted people who were going to be there for a while. After three years of prison life, I applied for a job in the gym and I got accepted as somebody who could just sweep up and put all the weights, barbells and medicine balls back in their correct place. It was a mediocre job which didn't get paid, but I enjoyed it as I could use any of the equipment – I had free access to it, which was like a benefit and, on some occasions, we had ladies come in from Modulo 1. Obviously, it was all sectioned off, but you could have a chance to talk to, or even flirt with them. Sometimes you could see prisoners from the other modules and that was good.

For some time, I took advantage of the prison courses that were on offer, anything to get a change in my routine. You could learn Spanish, so I took this and improved my knowledge of the language – I have always thought that it is good to learn other languages – I did well in French at school and came top. I enjoyed learning Spanish – when you are inside, and you have nothing else to do, you try to find things that fill the time – learning new skills. I also started the maths course with the Spanish people. Even though I knew the maths, I did it to help to pass the time and to keep my brain occupied. These courses were in the morning; it also helped to build relationships with the other prisoners who came in. You did whatever you could to eat into the time and you went to whatever classes were available.

I was in the gym everyday – the prison lady in charge was a very attractive young lady who was nice and friendly to me and one day she saw I did not have any trainers so she bought me some. It was a great gig to get! Most people wanted to get into the gym, firstly, because there was a nice-looking lady there and secondly you could get fit and do what you wanted to. I never took full advantage of it, but it was a nice situation. There were people who got work that paid a small amount of money. I didn't get any pay, as the gym was perceived to be an easy job and you didn't get paid for an easy job. But there were inmates who did get paid work and you would see them every morning in their blue boiler suits as they went off to the maintenance areas, or in the white suits for the kitchen – if you were given a suit, you would go to a specific part of the prison where you would have to work from morning right through till you came back for dinner. They would have their lunch separately, while working off-site or in an area such as maintenance, carpentry etc and they would get "pocket money" each week. So that was fine.

I did write a couple of letters to Pat, my old boss and drinking buddy from way back and directed my correspondence via the bar in Altea. I enjoyed writing the letters and didn't let on where I was but went into detail how my life had changed for the better since leaving the UK and how much I had changed physically and basically just waffled on and on, it passed the time and I enjoyed waiting for a reply which would come via the bar and sent to me in Modulo 3. Pat's letters were always lengthy and an enjoyable read. I would go every day to the post board to see if I had any mail, it became one of my highlights.

The days just rolled into months and the months rolled into years. It was the same thing every day, it was repetitive, the food was mediocre. However, there was one day when we were told that it was the day of celebration for the Catholic saint for prisoners – I do not remember which one as there are 26 listed by the Catholics as patron saints of prisoners!

On this one day, the prisons roll out nice food – it was the only day of the year when they gave us something different in the way of food! You might have a nice Boeuf Bourguignon – it was always a nice meal and well looked forward to by all the inmates.

I had been in prison for about 4 years by now and I remember once a Spanish shemale inmate came into the Modulo 3, a transgender person - a boy dressed as a girl, he looked like a girl, he walked like a woman and could dress as a woman. Actually, she was quite attractive with long straight dark hair and breasts. She got a lot of attention from everyone and was put in the men's prison as the authorities felt that it was not possible or practical to put him in the women's Modulo. I felt so sorry for that person, she got a lot of abuse, sexual harassment and sexual attention, including being raped. This was in 1995 and the world was not as informed and intuitive about this sort of situation as it is today.

There were a couple of guys who did turn up eventually about a year after I came in, who were big in drugs. These weren't your floor level entry drugs guys. They were like the main bosses. I won't give their names as they were Brits and they might still be alive. We got on with them straight away, but they were multi-millionaires. They told us about their lifestyle, their boats and villas, and you could tell from the way that they were, that they were the just normal people, I enjoyed their company.

They came in not knowing what to expect – it was their first time inside and they had stashed loads of 500 peseta notes, underneath the soles of their shoes, all around them – they had money coming through their accounts, but this was just to get them going! We had a great time with these guys as they were straight into their drugs and we had some serious smoking sessions with them.

Just thinking back now about prison, I took in more about every aspect of each day during my second time in jail as, obviously, I was there for a longer period of time. I remember the prison sounds, all the different cultures, the different nationalities that were in this prison. It was chaotic, the accents, the different languages, Mexicans, Brazilians, Argentinians, Columbians, Italians, Swedish, and a few Polish, plus, of course Spanish, a real mixed bag. The Spanish people loved their music and we could constantly hear them singing, especially the Gypsy singers or 'Gitanos' as they were referred to, they would sing all day, from dawn to dusk, Gypsy wailing songs - it was their way of escaping from their surroundings.

I remember that I used to listen to a little battery-powered radio that I had acquired from a former prisoner who had been released and I really appreciated it when I found a station that played only English music. I would listen to it for hours on end, until the batteries ran down. I used to try to recharge the batteries by leaving them by the grilled bars of the window so that they would warm up or buy new ones from the tuck shop. I would listen to anything on the radio, I particularly remember listening to Tasmin Archer's "Sleeping Satellite" and wishing I could be outside, free and enjoying this song in a bar.

That was one song that I remember from my time in prison. I've got it on my playlist now and every time I hear it, it takes me back to that time in the Spanish jail when I was listening to it, inside four walls in the courtyard area. There were other songs and even now when I hear them, they transport me back to that time. Music has always brought back memories for me. I didn't have a radio with me when I came to prison, it was left to me by another inmate with whom I got on. If ever someone left, they would leave whatever they didn't want to other inmates, that's just how it went.

Years earlier, I had a crush on a girl at my first job, she was a stunner. We all went out one night to a club and I remember having a chat and a drink at the bar and this same girl came up to me *"Would you like to dance, Sean?"* I was shy because she was a real beauty, same age as me. I went *"No, no"* but she wouldn't take no for an answer and said, *"Come on let's have a dance"* and, as we got down to the dance floor, the music changed, and this song came on - it was Simply Red's 'Holding Back the Years.' We just embraced and slow danced together, it was just like "Wow, can this night get any better?" The song played and we had the best dance ever and I did not want it to end but that was just one song that I remember. Whenever I hear it, I'm automatically transported back to 1986 on that dance floor and yes, I have that one on my playlist too.

Anyway, I digress slightly. Prison life was by far the hardest thing I've ever had to endure, it nearly drove me into becoming an insane drug addict. You were isolated, set apart from normal society and it was all so regimented. While it did give you a certain degree of discipline, it was something that I would never, ever advocate. Having said that, for me, it was probably the right thing at the right time because if it had not happened then, I was most definitely going in the wrong direction in my life and maybe without prison and this chapter in my life I might not have been alive by the time that I reached 30. I don't know.

Chapter 17 – Freedom!

I discovered later that my family were over the moon getting letters from me after not hearing from me for over five years; they were pleased and happy to learn I was working in a bar in Spain. Eventually my Dad and my two brothers came out to Alicante to try to find me to catch up and have a beer. Mom did not come. They went to the bar in Altea to see how I was doing. The lady to whom they spoke in the bar said, *"But he hasn't worked here since whenever."*

They said, *"That's strange, we have been getting letters from him saying he has been working here."*

I was told afterwards that she really did not know what to say. So, they found out that I was not working in the bar, I was not doing what I said I was doing! They must have thought this was really strange and must have been getting worried. The bar lady was obviously in a predicament and finally after a few minutes of head scratching she eventually said to my dad *"You might want to check out Fontcalent prison."*

One day, I think I was about four years into my sentence, I had a call over the speaker system that I had a visitor, someone had come to see me. I was amazed as I had not had any visitors since arriving, no-one from the Consulate, no-one had come to see me, I was left to my own devices. So, you can imagine that when I turned up at the visiting area and just walked in, not knowing what to expect, I was gob-smacked!

What changed my life for me was that day when my family came to see me, and they saw the condition I was in. When I went into Fontcalent, I was about 16 stone and I came out at just over 11 stone! I'd lost a lot of weight but when my family saw me, it was heart wrenching, I just felt so bad. I must have cast a long forlorn shadow and looked like a skeleton to them but we had a heartfelt emotional reconnection. I not going to lie there were tears. I was wearing baggy clothes and my skin was dry and I probably looked about five years older than I really was. I was just skin and bone, wearing unwashed clothes, my hair long and unkempt We had a long chat and they told me Mom had changed for the better, probably because I hadn't been there for five years.

They wanted to help me get out of there as quickly as possible and, on their return to England, my Dad spoke to his brother and my Uncle paid for a Spanish lawyer to see whether they could get me out, because I had done over half of my sentence – I'd done four years and three months of my eight years. Within two weeks of me seeing my family for the first time in nearly 5 years I got the news I was praying for. I remember the senior prison guard telling me one afternoon *"You are going to be let out tomorrow, you are going to be extradited back to England."*

I was given an expulsion notice that meant that I couldn't return to Spain for three years - not that I wanted to anyway, I was just glad that I was going home! I have been back on several occasions since but, obviously, at that time, I was just happy to be out. I remember leaving the prison – it was about 10 o'clock at night and it was dark. Everyone knew I was leaving that day, but they did not know when and neither did I.

When I was leaving, I got a rapturous round of applause as everyone began to bang against the steel bars with their metal cups and mugs. It was quite a loud exit, because I was well-known to so many of the prisoners, not just the odd British ones, but also other Europeans and indeed, some of the South Americans – I got on with most people, I didn't cause any problems, but I will never forget the whole Modulo giving me a huge send off. I was overwhelmed. I left my radio and pretty much all the stuff I had to my cell mates. It was very unusual and felt surreal to be leaving a place that I had called home for the past 4 years. It felt a bit like leaving the Big Brother house.

At the allotted time, I was taken to the airport and put on the plane by armed police while still in handcuffs. They took me to my seat and then uncuffed me, leaving me amid normal passengers, much to everyone's amazement and curiosity. They had timed it so that I went from the prison straight to the plane, there was no dilly-dallying around waiting for anything, no going to an hotel or anything, it was just straight out and on to the plane, which then took off straight away. They were definitely keeping an eye on me to ensure that I didn't cause any more problems.

Again, I was told I was not to return within three years. That was their duty done. I noticed the passengers were all wondering what the hell was going on, with this man being escorted on to their plane in handcuffs by armed police! I was flown to Gatwick, where I was met by my Dad and my two brothers – that was obviously a joyous moment, connecting back with my family after more than four years. It was all down to them coming over to that bar just to see me and it all moved on from there. I was very appreciative of the fact that they did come over for me, otherwise I would have had to serve my time and then been released back out into the world, but the fact that this lawyer got involved was a godsend really. He said, *"This guy needs to be released"* and the appeal for my release came just at the right time.

One positive that came out of this was that the Spanish had spelled my first name incorrect on all the legal documents. I was never bothered to mention it, they never had a passport to double check against. I always wondered whether my name linked to prison would come up under any searches on the Internet and it doesn't! For that reason, I was quite fortunate they messed up!

This was an interesting chapter in my life – I'm glad that it happened when it did because I believe that if it hadn't happened then, it might have happened at a later time, because I was on one of those paths in life when anything could happen. I do believe, however, that it happened at the right time for me. Once I had got this out of my system and now that I knew what it was like to go inside, especially in a high security foreign prison, I just knew that I never wanted my liberty or freedom to be taken away ever again. That was the measure of me, because I turned around and said I never want to revisit that situation. It's like drink-driving – I got caught for drink-driving once and I said after that – not being able to drive for two years – I never wanted that situation to happen again. Once it has happened you have to learn from that lesson.

To be fair, one of the first things that my brothers said to me, on the way home from Gatwick, was *"Mom has calmed down a lot since you left, Sean"*

In all honesty, I think that I was the irritation. They said, *"She has been great, she's been as good as gold!"*

I said, *"Do you think that Mom is going to be OK with me."*

Again, they said *"Yes, she has been really happy!"*

When I arrived home, she greeted me as warmly as her feelings would allow and, despite her welcome, there was a little bit of conflict initially. I had to sleep on the sofa because all the rooms had been redistributed while I was away, the bunk beds had gone, and my two brothers were still living at home. So, I ended up back on the sofa, which was not the best scenario, but it all came out in the wash.

Chapter 18 – Home Time!

I clearly remember coming home, I didn't have a job, I had no money and I was still living on the settee. However, more importantly, I was feeling jubilant, feeling free and feeling positive – I was young enough that I hadn't totally screwed up my life, I was only 25 and I was driven not to make the same mistake twice. I really believe to this day that I was destined to go to prison at some point in my life. I was just glad and rejoiced thereafter that it was sooner rather than later in my life – at least I felt that I had got the badness out of my system, a poison that I had to get rid of before it destroyed my life altogether.

After a few months from returning from Spain I was still cashless and getting bored. I was still young and I wanted to enjoy myself and to try and catch up a bit on lost time. I remember that, as a Catholic family, we used to go to church every Sunday evening. I would spend the whole of the service begging my oldest brother to lend me some money. He had a steady job at the time, and he was good at saving his own money. I would beg him from the moment the priest started the opening prayer till the moment the congregation filed out of the church *"Can you lend me a tenner? Can you lend me a tenner?"*

"No!"

"Can you lend me a tenner?" This mantra repeated itself for 45 minutes, until he finally relented – I don't think that he could take it any longer and coughed up! I think he ended up dreading going to church on a Sunday, but I used the

money unwisely and spent it down the pub, just socialising! Considering that I hadn't socialised for a nearly five years, I felt that I needed something to take my mind off my current situation and to celebrate my freedom.

I remember once, I was so desperate for cash that I went and asked my Granddad (my Mom's Dad) for some money. He was a very shrewd, wily old man who lived in Alum Rock, so I went over on the bus. He was always as frugal with his money as he was contemptuous of flagrant displays of generosity and wealth. I was his grandson and probably one of his greatest disappointments. I remember being quizzed by my Granddad for over an hour about what I was going to use the money for. I think that it was about £400 that I asked him for. I said I was looking to buy a car or something like that. In truth, I needed it to live on and for my socialising.

I was so desperate for cash. He must have asked me over a hundred questions about my current financial situation, until even he decided that only way to get rid of me was to make out a cheque. To this day, I remember him writing that cheque. It took him as long to write the cheque as it had taken for the whole of the previous conversation that we had just had! He made it feel tortuous – he wrote that cheque at a snail's pace, probably all the time wondering if he was making a bad decision. I remember every tear from his cheque book, from the top to the bottom took him an age. It was one excruciatingly slow rip after another. I could not wait to get out of there, and I knew I never wanted to relive this experience again or ever ask him for money again. He probably realised it too.

The cheque weighed heavy in my pocket all the way home and I wondered if the two or more hours that it had taken was worth the social trauma and embarrassment that

I would face in seeing him again, as I had promised him faithfully that I would pay him back in full in just a few weeks. He must have known that it would be a lot longer but, to his credit, he never mentioned it in company or in public. I just knew that he knew and that ate away at me – not only was I his oldest grandson but I was also his only godson. I met him a few times afterwards at social and family gatherings, he never said a word about it to me. I always felt bad at these occasions because a few of our family knew where I had been, and there was a black cloud hovering constantly above my head. My aunty - the nun with a PHD who was my mom's sister - pulled me to one side and said to me, "*Sean, you should try and keep a memoir or journal of your time in Spain to remember back, it might make interesting reading or a good book for when you are older.*" I never thought much about it, but she was right and so she planted a seed that has only taken about twenty-five years to mature!

I did repay my Grandad in full many years later, with interest, and the smile that I received from him was the greatest thanks that I could have received. No words were exchanged or spoken, just a gentlemanly nod and that was all I needed to know that I had done a small act to redeem myself in his good favour and the family fold.

I respected my Grandfather greatly. He was a sagely man who seemed to be able to look deep into the core of my spirit. He was just one of those people whom I totally adored, respected and I really wanted to emulate but I knew I was just a total disappointment to him. As I mentioned previously, I was just the black sheep of the family. My Mom was always telling him that I was just doing this and that, that I was getting myself into trouble or I was just going wayward and this was even before I had gone off the rails at far too young an age and I needed to make a man of myself. He had been retired about ten years at this stage, but he had saved every penny. I always just remember that he did not like to splash the cash.

The time that I asked him for the money was about two months after I had come back from Spain. He already knew a lot about my prison sentence, as did a few close family members, so that made asking him for the money that much harder. Asking someone for money when you have a clean slate is easy, but when you know that you are asking someone who knows your background, it's ten times worse.

At this time, I was casually looking around to see if there were any jobs available, but I admit that I was not taking this very seriously. One weekend, I wanted to go out with a friend up town, but I had no money and no decent clothes. I remember sneaking into Mike's bedroom to borrow some clothes from his wardrobe. He had always had a good eye for clothes and his clothes were a lot more stylish than the ones that I ever had – he had been slimmer than me but when I came back from Spain, we were much the same size.

I remember sneaking into my brother's bedroom to borrow his clothes, only to find that he had multiple-padlocked his own wardrobe! He had done this, most probably, because he knew I would try to get to his clothes. He was always thinking ahead. I went and found a Philips screwdriver and unscrewed the screws in the padlock hinge mechanism and went on to borrow some smart clothes for my night out. I remember putting the screws back in place and didn't think any more of it. Before he woke up, I replaced all the clothes I had borrowed so as not to cause a row.

However, the next day, all hell broke loose when my brother accused me of taking his smartest shirt and jeans. I denied all knowledge as I thought that he would not be able to prove it, only to be advised by my brother that he knew that the padlock had been tampered with as he had pre-set all the screw heads in an exact horizontal and vertical position, so not only did he padlock it, but he also knew how he had left the screws. I could not believe that my brother had pre-positioned all the screws and had me so banged to rights! I was so dumb! He had an abundance of common sense, which obviously suits him now, as he is in the police force.

After about four months of living on the settee, my Mom's patience was wearing extremely thin, the increase in tension was palpable and, once more, was beginning to have a negative impact on family life, and the karma within. I remember my Mom coming home from work one day with a cold dish of meat and gravy and, with an impassioned plea to get a job, if not for my sake then for her own sake and her sanity. I think that she had had enough of coming down in the morning and seeing me just lying there on the settee! I was there and I was just an on-going aggravation.

About six months after me coming home, my Mother left home. My Dad and her had been having marital problems for years prior to me coming home but I suppose my return was just the straw that broke the camel's back. She left us and shacked up with her first ever boyfriend whom she had bumped into randomly one night in the Irish Centre, in Digbeth, Birmingham. It transpired that she had been seeing him on and off for a while. I think that my Dad knew she was having an affair behind his back but either turned a blind eye to it or didn't know how to deal with the situation. I did not feel the total weight of responsibility for this as the affair had started prior to me returning home from Spain. This was probably why my brothers had told me Mom had changed and was happy. My return may have been the catalyst, but Mom was already having this affair with this guy whom she had known in Ireland about thirty years earlier.

I think that my Mother always thought that the she knew best and, after 25 years of married life to my father, she upped sticks and flew the nest. I think deep down, my Father had a happier life without my Mother and to be fair they seemed to get on better when not living together. She was unhinged at the best of times and totally apocalyptic at the worst. She could throw a tantrum over the smallest thing and she had the shortest fuse.

It was shortly after Mom left home that I hit rock bottom again. I was so desperate for money. That was when I started to steal money from my Dad. I used to rifle through his work jacket pocket for any loose change so that I could buy myself a beer or two. I felt like a real scumbag doing this to him, especially as he was the only one who had only ever shown me love. He was also the one who had led the drive to find out where I was and then to bring me home. He must have known that pound coins were going missing from his coat pocket and who was the culprit, but he never raised the issue with me. I am glad to say that after I got back on to my feet, that terrible habit stopped. Upon reflection, I know now that if I had asked him outright for the money, he would just have given it to me but, at the time, I was scared he might say no and I was also afraid of the subsequent repercussions.

I didn't realise at the time that finding that booze in the cupboard all those years ago was the beginning of the end for my parent's marriage, being made to face up to the situation was the final nail in the coffin for my Dad. He just did not know how to cope with my Mother and her chaotic episodes. She was in torment and was obviously suffering mentally as well, alcohol and pills were her comfort blanket. When it came to my parent's marriage, it was becoming increasingly obvious to everyone that my Mother was no longer content or happy being a part of our family and being married to Dad but, despite my Dad's best efforts, it was all to no avail. She filed for divorce shortly afterwards.

My mother always believed, right to the end of her life, that the grass was always greener elsewhere, even though it seldom was. She walked out on the family unit. She just got up and left. She was not happy, and I think she just felt she was making things worse. She thought she had found romance and love again with an old boyfriend, whom she had known long before she met my Dad. I think she just wanted to be loved and to feel love again and was prepared to do whatever she thought best to achieve that goal.

In some ways, Mom leaving was for the best, it brought life at family level to a norm and though I shouldn't really say this, she became someone else's problem. I began to heal and started gradually to feel better about myself, even though I put back on almost three stone in weight in just under a year from coming back and felt a little self-conscious about my weight gain and appearance. My Mom and me, we got on better with her from a distance, when there was about five miles between us. I used to visit her to make sure she was ok, and we had pleasant, almost normal conversations. She seemed to genuinely seem interested in what I had been doing and if there was any gossip. I didn't want to say that the only gossip was, probably, the neighbours talking about her leaving Dad and shacking up with another man! She always made out that things were just fantastic and life was great. Whether that was true or not I am unsure. I actually bonded better with her when she was living away from us. She became like a family member you visit on a regular basis. She became more friendly and welcoming when our visits were kept to about 30-40 minutes, almost like a grandparent would feel when they see their grandchildren I suppose. She seemed happier in herself and that made me feel happy too. It was like she had been diagnosed and then cured of cancer and was now on the road to recovery, if that makes sense.

When I look back, I realise now that Mom was totally barmy, she lived by a different set of rules to the rest of us. She had a different concept of normality than probably 99% of the population and always thought she knew best, even if it was totally ludicrous. I remember one occasion when I was about 25 years old and I was discussing my weight gain and appearance and self-confidence; I was paranoid about the way I looked. I was visiting her and popped around to have a chat when she suddenly said to me "*Sean, I need you to come with me.*"

I said, "*Where are we going?*"

"*I might have the answer to your prayers*" she said with a smirk and a knowing look and took me into Birmingham city centre on a No 50 bus. My Mom was into all these quack doctors and stuff and she took me to this doctor in a back street, just a stone's throw from the Bullring. He had a small office in a large commercial building. His name was handwritten outside the front door on the list of businesses that occupied the building, plus an entry doorbell. After walking up a few flights of stairs, there was a second buzzer outside his office to let you in.

Mom said, "*This is my son, can you prescribe him the same pills you gave me last time?*"

This suited up and smart looking doctor looked me over and asked me some basic health questions, probably to try and act all legitimate and doctor-like. But, after only a handful of questions he did what my Mom had requested, I don't know why, I don't even know if he was a real doctor or not. I was shocked and thought this was all a bit surreal. His office seemed bona-fide, his appearance seemed genuine, but something felt off kilter. I knew Mom used to pop a few pills in the morning from her medicine box and mixing it with a glass of whiskey and think it was fine, she lived by her own rules. She must have been getting her pills from this guy.

He signed off on Mom's request, Mom handed him some money and he produced from his bottom drawer a large plastic container full of tablets and handed them to her. These tablets were just super-charged speed pills, similar to what you would get at any rave! I was literally buzzing for hours. I could run 100 metres in about 10 seconds (give or take about 20 seconds!). I would take one and, very quickly, I was washing my Dad's car, I was hoovering the house from top to bottom, rearranging all the cupboards, washing and ironing all the clothes in the laundry basket. I was just in constant hyperactive mode and I think my Mom thought all this extra spent energy would have the weight falling off me. She must have thought that this would have the desired effect and was the answer to my prayers – just run around the house! That was how my Mom's brain worked. She meant well but thought the answer to me getting thin was to get me drugs!

Chapter 19 – Currying Favour

It was at this time in my life, I think, that I was becoming addicted to alcohol and dependent upon it, just like my Mom, and it resonated in my mind that I was becoming a replica of her. That sent me into a bit of a tizzy, and it made me feel worse about myself – am I going to go off the rails, just like her? I was coming home drunk and waking up needing a beer – the hair of the dog! I was mixing with some hard, Irish drinkers who could drink a young drinker like me under the table. Furthermore, I needed the money to buy rounds and that was why I stole from my Dad. Looking back, I feel really embarrassed about this part of my life – however, I would prefer to look good in front of my new drinking buddies rather than to be labelled a thief by my own father. I think that, with my Mom no longer there to discipline me, I had convinced myself that I had a free pass to do as I pleased.

I was spiralling downwards and sinking and needed to get myself sorted out before it was too late. I too started on the early morning miniatures – there was some part of me that resonated with how my Mom had been and, obviously, the apple doesn't fall too far from the tree. I thought that maybe this is my destiny, but there was a loud bell ringing, that I needed to rethink my lifestyle before it was too late.

I found my first job after leaving Fontcalent Prison while scouring the jobs section in the local Thursday edition of the Evening Mail newspaper. It seemed too good to be true and read something like:

£££ -Apply Today, Immediate Start-£££
-Fantastic Salary Opportunities
-No Previous Sales Experience
-Be Your Own Boss
-Call This Number Now!

Well, I was desperate for a job and they seemed keen to give me an opportunity. I called and they arranged for me to go into their office for an interview. This all seemed fine and above board. When I had the interview, they seemed quite keen to get me started, which was a surprise as I obviously hadn't any previous sales experience. They said that, if I was interested in the job, I could start the next day and I would be doing selling. I thought why not?

I was advised to meet someone the next day and was given a collection point. I thought to myself 'Oh, that's nice, they are collecting me and taking me to work. This is a company that cares about its employees.' The next day I met up with Jez in his Escort XR3I and he had about three other passengers. I had been told to look smart and presentable, so I turned up in my brother's suit, which he didn't know I had borrowed. We had coffee in a local coffee shop and Jez who was the organiser said that we had a certain area to cover in seven hours and we would be canvassing door to door for voucher sales on certain takeaways, such as local Pizza, Pasta and Chinese restaurants. We sold a laminated voucher card to the customer, which then gave them discount on orders purchased from the takeaway.

Up to this point, until Jez had outlined the specifics, I had no real idea what my job entailed. I was only advised that I needed to be good at sales and the wages were sales driven so the more I sold, the more I could earn. When the full realisation hit me that I was doing door to door, I was shocked, as this was never made clear to me. I suppose, with hindsight, I was so desperate for a job that I didn't really drill down too much when I was being interviewed. I was just so chuffed to be offered the job on the spot. Unbeknown to me - and something I hadn't realised at the time - was that if I had a pulse, I had the job the moment I sat down!

Anyway, the day started off rubbish with me having the door slammed in my face and people shouting at me to "Do One!" and sometimes they just dropped the F-Bomb on me and closed the door with a loud bang. I was not enjoying this experience one bit, especially as it was raining, and I'd not planned on this being outside work and never thought to bring an umbrella with me. I must have walked anywhere between five and ten miles that day, all around this new estate. I hated every second of this job, as I felt I'd been hoodwinked into doing it under false pretences. However, I hadn't signed any contract so I suppose I was the fool to jump in without any thought of what I might be doing. I was so desperate, normally I like to research a company or do my homework on exactly what the job would entail, but I was so desperate. I swore I would never make the same mistake again. I put this one day down as a lesson learned.

At the end of the day, when we all met up at Jez's car to pool our cash and to see what we had all earned, I was embarrassed to have only brought in £10 for one Voucher Card sold. Jez, I think must have felt sorry for me and gave me a fiver for my day's troubles and said that I would do a lot better the next day. I never saw Jez again, I had decided there and then, in his claustrophobic XR3I with Jez and three other random guys, that Door-to-Door Sales was not my thing. I think it's a hard job and is purely sales driven, but there must be better ways to earn a living.

When I mentioned my Door-to-Door nightmare to my mother on one of week up meetings, I think she was pleased that I had tried and failed rather than not tried at all. This must have pleased her as she said she would ask around at her place of work to see if anyone knew of any jobs going. I was surprised when the next day she phoned me and said she might have a job for me.

The job that my Mother had found for me was in a nightclub and the hours were long, but I was glad to be out of the house and having the opportunity to earn some money. In retrospect, this was the worst possible place for a young and vulnerable alcoholic to work – for that was what I had become. Being surrounded day and evening with all forms of alcohol – beers and spirits – and being permanently in the company of customers who, quite frequently would offer to buy me a drink, was simply putting too much temptation in front of me at a time when I had no wish to refuse it.

I enjoyed the banter of working behind the bar in the nightclub. When I had lived in London, I had worked in a pub and had enjoyed the craic with the punters. It was fun being back in that kind of environment, and I had my self-esteem back and I looking ok having consumed most of mom's crazy pills. I was 25 and the bar work was socially rewarding, financially rewarding and emotionally fulfilling as I was meeting some flirtatious ladies! It definitely made for a happier home life, despite still living on the settee.

I always used to leave the nightclub around two or three in the morning and, on my travels home, I used to see homeless people in back doorways or factory alcoves near the club. Whenever I saw someone, I always engaged with them as I remembered all those lonely, cold nights that I had spent in their situation on the streets of London, Brussels and Alicante, having taken out my bus fare home, I would hand over whatever change I had left in my pocket or my duffel coat at that time. It might not have been much, but it was more than they had. You hear stories that these people are just using or abusing the system; trust me, I know from my own sad experience that the majority are not. They are stuck in a rut and need community-support, certainly most of them do not want to continue to live rough.

One night after leaving work I was approached by a homeless guy, quoting a pre-rehearsed speech including squad number, rank and unit numbers in a soldier-like manner – *"I'm Corporal 931149, Leicester 31st Rifle Regiment, I have absconded from duty, gone AWOL, and need my train fare home, Sir."*

I know it was a cover story and that he was a homeless guy and was desperate for money, just like I was – society has failed them for whatever reason, so they have ended up on the streets. I gave him all the change I had in my pocket. I never turn a blind eye as I was once in exactly the same position and I always try to help out where I can, even if it is just to listen to their story and to find out how they ended up on the streets. A sympathetic ear, even. For a homeless person it might just be nice to have a friendly conversation. I always remember "Snakes and Ladders" where one day, through no fault of your own, you fall down a rung or two. I can tell you from personal experience that it's no fun living rough on the streets.

The nightclub was built over two storeys. I was working on the top tier in the nightclub with the dance floor and DJ, the middle floor was the bar, comfortable seating and a few gambling machines while, in the basement was an authentic Indian restaurant with a good reputation for quality meals. I always enjoyed walking home with a Naan bread filled with a delicious meat curry and chutney at the end of any of my shifts. One day, they were short of staff in the restaurant and had asked for some help from the nightclub bar staff. I think that most of the staff would have turned up their noses at the prospect of moving down to the basement, where the glamour and shine was not to everyone's taste. No-one wanted to work in the restaurant, as it was not so glamorous as being a waiter in the bar, so I volunteered, as I enjoyed eating the food. I knew that the tips would be good as they shared the pot at the end of each evening; the staff were easy to get on with and they seemed to have a good laugh. As you can imagine, it was unusual to have your food and drinks orders taken by a young white chap, but it did not bother me in the slightest. I got far more tips than when I was working in the nightclub and life started getting better.

From then on, I worked in the restaurant on a much more regular basis, starting in the nightclub for the first few hours and then moving downstairs from about 10pm until about 2am. I remember serving some famous people there, as we were in Birmingham City Centre and so attracted some high-profile customers. I became a decent waiter. On one occasion, I was due to be working in the restaurant when a party of about eight arrived just after midnight, as I arrived downstairs to start my night shift. We gave them a table and seated them, and I was looking after their drinks order, when one of the diners asked me, out of the blue, what my position was in this establishment.

Now this was one of those moments in your life that you must take advantage of - when opportunity knocks, you must be ready. I was slightly surprised for a moment and was taken aback, and this gave me a few moments to consider what was happening. I told him that I was the Assistant Manager. I was dressed all in black, with dark black turtle neck top and stonewashed blue jeans, as I normally worked upstairs in the bar, so my casual attire stood out from the waiters in their white shirts and black trousers.

He looked suitably impressed and said, *"I am the manager of a pub and am looking for a good assistant manager, would you consider coming to work for me?"*

"I might if the pay is right" I replied confidently.

Chapter 20 – Blagging

Remember that only I could help me! That me telling this random customer that I was the actual Assistant Manager was a little white lie, but what harm did it do? I let it wait for a few days before I called him, as I didn't want to seem too eager or too desperate, but we arranged an interview. Before I turned up, though, I did my research thoroughly. I went into Birmingham Central Library and I read up and studied books on management, retail and liquor licensing laws. I read as much as I could about hospitality, staffing, product lines, health and safety, anything that I thought to be prudent or of value. I also went to my local pub and started talking to the Assistant Manager, just to find out what his job included. He gave me a good piece of advice – it's always good to have a decent SWOT (Strengths, Weaknesses, Opportunities and Threats) analysis done.

I found out in advance of the interview what the local breweries and pub chains were doing to drum up business. I just phoned them up and asked them if they had any forthcoming events lined up and I was given some key dates on DJ nights, quiz nights and any forthcoming special occasions that they had lined up, such as Valentine's Days, Mothers' days – in other words, basic information that I thought might prove to be of interest.

Anyway, I felt prepared for the interview and I presented a good case for him to hire me. My prospective employer was quite an authoritative person in his character and his mannerisms – just think of an angry Jeremy Clarkson, but on steroids! I remember him telling me at the time, 'just remember I can be a total bastard!' I am a firm believer that, if you are going to blag, then at least come up with something that can be substantiated so that you can be perceived as being 100% credible and so as not to waste anyone's time. It could have been a brief and pointless interview if I had tried to get through the interview without having done my research.

In the event, I must have done something right as he offered me the job! I'd blagged a job from being a nobody barman/waiter on a pittance of a salary to an Assistant Manager for a bar and restaurant! I have blagged a few jobs but this was the best one I blagged. If I had told him at the time that I was just the drinks waiter he would have probably tipped me a fiver and nothing more would ever have been said. It turned out that he had a large pub with a restaurant that sat about 100 covers. I was immediately impressed with the set up and the location and, most of all, the hours. I knew nothing at all about management, supply lines, profit and loss, margins or even staff rotas, other than what I had read in the library. I had had to blag him!

I learned a hell of a lot from this boss. He was very strict and liked everything to be precise. If a single light bulb was blown and it hadn't been changed, he would notice it straightaway and dish out a reprimand! He always demanded 100% commitment, which ensured a great work ethic from everybody that worked for him. I got the job and it was a real learning experience working for him because he was fanatical about everything being spot on. You knew when he was going to arrive in the restaurant because he did everything by the second. Everyone was shit scared of him.

I was now working for Clarkson, I was still only 25, but I was on the edge of the precipice of alcoholism – I was drinking a lot – too much. Truthfully, I was in the wrong place. I was drinking a lot in the evening with the regulars. I also developed a worrying gambling problem – which was the gruesome twosome! There was a bookie's shop directly over the road from the pub and basically, at lunchtime, or in a quiet moment, I would pop over the road and bang my money on the nag! It was always the horses. I don't know but I think that this was just the way that my life was evolving after everything that had gone before. It was my release mechanism. I don't know why I turned to alcohol and gambling, but it just felt like an enjoyable vice. That was how I saw it at the time.

I had the sort of personality that enjoyed the high that came from drinking alcohol and betting at the bookies on the horses. It was in the days before on-line gambling and so everything was more exciting, going to the bookies to watch the horseracing. I used to go there in my lunch hour and just sit and enjoy the thrill of watching the racing. I always used to smile at the name over the door "turf accountants", I always thought that it was a strange name as it made it sound much more professional.

I knew it was wrong to be constantly betting and drinking, I just believed that it was socially acceptable – after all, I wasn't the only person doing it! I always felt that I was in control of it rather than the other way around, namely the gambling and drinking being in control of me. I just used to feel that the answer was at the bottom of a bottle of lager – for that 5-10 minutes after a drink, I would feel OK, but then it all kicked in and I started to feel bad, so I would need more alcohol to get me back on to a level playing field. Being in the pub trade meant that I was always near my demons. To be honest, it was the worst place to be, but I later realised that a lot of alcoholics either end up in bar work or, alternatively, bar work creates a lot of alcoholics!

I remember while I was growing up watching lots of TV programmes in the 1970s and early 1980s, films where the actors, usually the hero or the main guy, used to drink Scotch or Bourbon straight from the tumbler, knocking it back in one smooth action; I used to think that it looked quite cool. John Wayne used to call for a neat one and knock it straight back at the bar, so I used to think, well if he can do it, so can I! I never realised at the time that the people who were drinking were, in reality, drinking alcohol-coloured water, or cold tea – it wasn't really alcohol! That is why it had no effect upon them whatsoever. Alcohol is very addictive, and I obviously had an addictive type of personality, but I could not stand the man that it made me. I never lapsed into violence, but I do remember having bouts of total memory loss or at least fragmented memories.

As an example, I remember one evening, after my pub shift ended, I headed up to the City and went to a casino where I was a member. I had been drinking a bit after work and I thought it would be fun. I was on my own and headed to my favourite place at the roulette table. I was hitting some lucky numbers and must have won a couple of grand, which was a lot back 1995. I was feeling in a jubilant and intoxicated mood and felt on a real big high. I remember being chatted up by a woman at the bar and we had a few drinks. I thought that my luck was in when she offered to take me home – as you can probably gather - and as I found out after we had sexual relations, that she was a hooker on the lookout for intoxicated souls such as me.

She started demanding payment and I refused to pay her because she had neither told me there was a payment required, or if she did, I was too inebriated to hear it nor any pimp to back her up. She tried to bar my way out of her apartment. I tried desperately to make for the door, but she was having none of it. She was going full tilt crazy in my face and at this point grabbed hold of a short-bladed knife from inside a table drawer in the hall way. Nothing sobers you up quicker than seeing someone shouting and screaming at you while pointing a knife at you! When she realised that no monetary exchange was going to happen, she stabbed her knife with force straight into my right lower arm. I saw the blood dripping straight away from my arm out of my jacket sleeve, even though I was still quite drunk I felt the pain immediately and was highly alarmed.

While I was trying to attend to the blood situation, she was desperately trying to pull out the wads of money that I had in my jacket pocket. Our bodies entangled for a second time that evening, my money was falling out of my pocket and my blood was dripping down from my arm. I remember pushing her away, grabbing the cash while trying to take the knife from her and to make my exit. The knife fell to the floor, but she kept up her physical attack, repeatedly hitting me, while threatening to call the police. I was so alarmed that I kept telling her to call them. She was like a screaming banshee!

I remember picking up all the money which, by now was covered in blood, and stuffing it back in my pockets while running as fast as I could out of her apartment. She gave chase, shoeless, while shouting and screaming. I remember running to a street corner telephone box and found safety and sanctuary behind the red door, while she caught up with me and started to hammer with her fists on the glass panels.

I picked up the telephone receiver and she saw me and heard me calling the police. On seeing me do this, she seemed to calm down and begged me to give her some money just to go away. I told her that she was a lunatic and that the police would be here shortly. She was barefooted with hardly any clothes on. She had no knife, but I was in a phone box with blood all over my jacket. I felt that I had a strong enough story if any police were to turn up. Finally, she cut her financial losses and ran off and that was the last I ever saw of her.

I was still feeling panicked, as I had just been stabbed by a hooker and I stayed in the telephone kiosk, for perhaps 10 minutes, before legging it. I certainly didn't want her back clothed with any backup! I went straight to A&E to get myself disinfected and stitched up. I cannot remember the exact story that I told them about what had happened to me – it was only a single stab wound but I still have the scar to this day.

It was an awkward conversation the following day, when I took about £2,000 in blood-stained notes into my local NatWest branch to deposit into my account. I remember the shock on her face and the bank teller looking at me and then looking at the notes and then looking back at me with alarm and confusion. Although I had steadied up a bit from the previous night, I must still have looked a right sight! My eyes were still bloodshot from the booze, I had bruises to my head and face from the punches and only had a patchy story to tell her.

I said that I had cut myself quite badly shaving – why I would be wet shaving over a bank roll of £2,000 goodness only knows! I don't think that she believed a word of it – I think that she was more worried that I had HIV or something similar and that she might catch it from me through the money. She referred it to her manager and eventually they did accept the notes. I think that she felt compelled to do so just to get rid of me and because she knew that I had a bank account with them. Whenever I went back to the casino after that, I always kept a watchful eye open but, thankfully, I never did spot that lady of the night again.

We had regular entertainment nights, with DJ's, at our pub and these nights were good. We had plenty of "Happy Hours" and we had a great melting pot of regulars from all works of life. We used to have "Lock-ins." We had a nice group of regulars and, at the end of the night, we would sometimes have a stop-over. Whoever was in the lock-in, we knew who they were, we trusted them, they were all over the age of 40, these were gentlemen. Most of them had their own businesses.

I was constantly drinking, but I tried to keep it low key. I wasn't drinking pints, I would drink vodka and soda water or gin and tonic, anything that was water coloured. I remember the turning point was when one group started coming into the pub, they were basically a group of thugs, they all worked together. The group went by a certain name, but I won't mention it as they weren't the friendliest bunch! Until then, we had had a great pub but then they started to create an underlying feeling – an unsociable group of drinkers and a nasty bunch of individuals. They didn't cause fights in the pub, but, if anyone came up to them and challenged them, they would immediately start throwing tables, chairs or anything else to hand. So, if a fight was going to happen, they were always in the middle of it. They were a major cause for concern to me and the rest of the staff, they needed handling.

However, Clarkson was only interested in bottom line profits, as his bonus was volume sales-related, and this group spent loads. They wouldn't come in and order a round of drinks, they would come in and order crates of bottled beer which they then took to their corner. They used to pay, but at the end of the week, or at the end of the month. The staff and the rest of the clientele used to see them being handed all these crates with no money being exchanged. My gaffer said that they paid him up at the end of the week or the month.

I kept telling him that they were driving out all our regulars, but he didn't care as long as we were hitting targets. I was worried as, on several occasions when it kicked off, we had to call the police and the pub began to get a bad reputation. I knew that the root of the problem was the presence of this group of thugs. I dreaded it every time that I saw them entering the pub and started to tell them that they would be barred if it started off again. There were eight or nine of them, but they were menacing, most of them were skinheads who could handle themselves and preferred to be left alone. I subsequently found out that they had been barred from many other pubs in the area. They never listened or just did not care, and they felt quite immune to it all. I don't think that they were necessarily looking for trouble, but trouble had a way of finding them.

Over the previous six-month period, the pub and restaurant had gone from being a family-friendly establishment to a fighting frenzy and a no-go area for a lot of the locals. I wasn't paid enough to be involved in all this and my boss kept turning a blind eye. I already needed alcohol just to get me through a shift, a feeling that was exacerbated when this group turned up. My staff kept asking me what I was going to do about them, but I didn't have any answers. The staff were very intimidated by all this and, when it kicked off, they would simply hide.

The worst fight was one night when it spilled over into the restaurant, as people would be dining, relaxing and just having an enjoyable meal and then it kicked off, and it was carnage, upsetting everyone. Fights are like wildfire; they don't just contain themselves in one area and they just used to spill out all over the place. Customers just wanted to come out for a quiet drink and a bite to eat and did not want to get caught up in all this unpleasantness.

After it had all settled down once the police had turned up, I said to my boss that, after this, he had to act immediately with these guys or else he was going to lose staff and trade. The staff were scared, and, at this point, the boss just did not care and just shrugged his shoulders and proceeded to walk away, I was livid.

But the answer soon came to me! My boss was due to go on his annual break and, as was customary, I had his upstairs living quarters while he was away so that I was on the premises. On the eve of his going away, a fight kicked off and, in the middle of it, one of the guys in the group picked up a brass beer tray from the counter and swung it. As it swung, it accidentally connected with the head of one of the bar staff. Normally, they only attacked their own group and never the staff, as this would result in the police being involved. Being hit by the bar tray knocked the lad out. I said to my boss that, after this, he had to act immediately with these guys.

Over the previous six-month period, the pub and restaurant had gone from being a family-friendly establishment to a fighting frenzy and a no-go area for all the locals. They just wanted to come out for a quiet drink and did not want to get caught up in all this unpleasantness.

On one particularly busy evening where both the bar and restaurant were jam packed, this fight was a bad one. It involved about 20 grown men and brought back déjà vu to when I was back in the prison yard. In the middle of the fight, one of the guys in the group picked up a brass beer tray from the counter and swung it. As it swung, it accidentally connected with the head of one of the bar staff who was bravely trying to call the police. Normally, they only attacked the people who caused them a problem and never the staff, as this would result in the police being involved. Being hit by the bar tray knocked the poor lad out and he needed hospital treatment. I also took one for the team and had been thumped hard in the head and felt the pain and a growing golf ball size lump on my forehead. I'd never even been hit in prison and now I felt more scared than I had been when inside. The staff were scared, and, at this point, the boss just did not care as he was about to go on holiday and was already in holiday mood – any confrontation at this point was out of the question. I was livid.

The next morning, he told me to look after the place while he and his family were away, said his goodbyes to all the staff and just pissed off. I was left in a situation where all the staff were about to walk out and Armageddon ensuing! Before the pub opened that morning, I had a sit-down meeting with all the staff and with all the managers of the relevant departments, catering, bar etc. My boss had gone and had left me to sort out the problem. I had a deputy manager – it was quite a big pub - but I was the acting manager and we had to decide what we were going to do.

Each of the departmental managers was saying that all their staff were unhappy and were worried about what might happen while the boss was away. AJC, the boss, was quite a strong character and perhaps they thought that if he was there, he might be able to do something if it all kicked off again. AJC was a stocky, bulldog-sort of man who could handle himself. With him out of the equation, it was like a cattle market. The staff were worried and said to me "*What are you going to do, because this is not a situation that we can tolerate for two weeks?*" They were already to walk out.

My solution involved bringing in temporary reinforcements. I couldn't handle this bunch on my own, so I phoned up my Area Manager and said "*He's off and we have an issue with an unruly group who are causing problems, its hitting profits and unless we do something all of the staff are going to walk out.*"

"*What do you want me to do?*"

"*I think that we should bring in some temporary doormen.*"

He said, "*Well, do whatever you think best.*"

There was only one lot of doormen that I knew in the area that would be up for the challenge to deal with this bunch of lads. They weren't youngsters who were off on a few drinks, they were hard nuts. The hardest doormen at that time belonged to a well-known hard guy, who had a reputation for sending doormen who could look after themselves. These bouncers were heavy duty and were not intimidated by the thought of pushing a fight outside in order to ensure the safety of the staff and customers – exactly what I needed at the time! Obviously with my boss on holiday, I was in charge and I wasn't paid enough to deal with the situation without backup.

My Area Manager signed off on it and said "*Do whatever you need to do, Sean. Just keep the pub safe until your boss comes back.*"

The staff were on the verge of walking out, so I felt that hiring these guys was my only option. The group of doormen came at a premium price, around £2,000 per week, which was a lot of money in those days, but I felt that it was justifiable in order to put a good business back on the rails. The doormen were made aware that their primary function was to keep this group of guys out of the pub and to keep any fight out of the building and to never let them interfere with business. These doormen used to come with corkscrews in their hands and I remember that they were on all the entry doors, but on the first night, the group slipped in through the back.

I said to my Bar Manager *"Flag that doorman over there"*.

We didn't have pictures of them, but the doormen needed to know who they were – we had just told them that we would let them know when they arrived. The Bar Manager ran over to the doorman and said, *"This is the group that we don't want in the pub."*

I followed up behind the Bar Manager and the doorman. The doorman straightaway said, *"You are not coming in!"*

The Group turned around and started swearing at him, saying *"Who do you think you are?"* to which he replied, *"I am entry and you lot are not coming in!"*

They turned around and said to him – and I remember it to this day – *"We will not cross this threshold if you belong to a certain organisation. If we know your employer, then we won't come over."*

I didn't know what they were on about, but the doorman simply said a certain well-known gangster man's name and said, *"I am one of his guys"*.

Upon hearing this, the Group turned around and straightway walked out. This guy meant business - he was like the Birmingham Mafia. We kept the doormen on site for the two weeks while the Boss was away – it cost the company over four grand, but it meant that we had a business for him to come back to. When he came back, he saw that we had the same staff as when he left, and he must have thought that this was alright, until he went up to the accounts and saw how much had come out of the business.

"What are these costs, these wages?"

When he saw what I had spent on wages, I told him that I had got the OK from up above, he wasn't happy about it. He said, *"I can't believe that you did that, you should never have done that."*

I said *"Well, you didn't leave me with any other options. The staff had threatened to walk out. It kicked off the night before you left, so what did you expect me to do? I simply did not have any other choice if we were to protect the pub and its business."*

We had a massive argument and he said to me "Y*ou just did the wrong thing."*

I replied *"Well, you have a business to come back to, haven't you?"*

I felt like an ungrateful babysitter – the kids were all there, but he wasn't happy with the way that things were. On top of which it was four grand out of his bottom line! So, I'd had enough and took the bunch of keys, threw them at him and said *"Stick these up your ass! I've had enough so you can find someone else to do the work."* As it was the end of my shift I just walked out and that was the end of my period in the pub trade.

I had been working long hours for Clarkson, from early in the morning when I sorted out the beer cellar until the early hours of the following morning, when everyone had gone home. When I left there, I needed to find work, I'd managed to save enough to buy a car and had saved a bit of money but not enough to keep me going as I was keen to wait for the swelling to reduce so that I could hunt for a less traumatic and scary job After quitting the pub, I carried on drinking and gambling, but obviously, not to the same level, firstly because I did not have the same exposure to them but, more importantly, I didn't have the funds coming in.

During the next two or three weeks I was in a quiet zone while I tried to dry out from the drink and the gambling and to work out what my next move was going to be. What do I do next? I was 25, I had no money and no future – again! Back to Ground Zero, I had found the bottom rung on the snakes and ladders board yet again!

Chapter 21 –
A Game Changer!

A few months prior to leaving the pub trade while I was still working for Clarkson, a chance meeting happened. Two friendly faces from my past just happened to walk in for a bite to eat one lunchtime. It was a total shock to the system but a really pleasant surprise. I hadn't seen them for several years - it was Joe and Dave from my very first Insurance job.

I went *"Oh my God, what on Earth are you guys doing here?!"*

They worked locally and had just walked in on the off chance for a lunchtime meal; I sat them down at a quiet table, and made sure they enjoyed a nice meal and beer, on the house! I couldn't believe it and was so pleased to see them as they brought back such happy memories. We caught up on old times and talked for ages, it was really nice to see them. I then kept in touch with them, because obviously now, I knew where they worked.

I asked how they were doing. Joe had been at this local insurance brokers for 10 or 15 years, having been the Office Manager, and he was now one of the Owners. I was blown away – it was obviously well deserved, and I was over the moon for both of him and Dave had recently joined him as a Sales Manager. They had their lunch and left but we agreed that we would stay in touch, now that we had met up again. – they had stayed in insurance and were now working together but they had gone their separate ways and then, somehow, had joined up again recently, how fate plays her hand!

It was another of those fateful moments when I just happened to be in the right place at the right time. If it had not been my shift or if I had been on my lunch or just anywhere else, I would never have bumped into them. After they had gone, I never really thought much more about it. However, I did insure my car with them as I thought that they would give me a good deal. The whole event was quite a fortuitous meeting and turned out to be a real game changer!

Shortly afterwards, having thrown my keys at my old boss and having walked out of the pub, I was looking round for a new opportunity. At home, we used to have the Evening Mail and I used to go through the management advertisements as I felt that I now had management experience and started looking for management roles. I always remember seeing an advertisement for a vacancy for as an Assistant Contract Manager for a catering company that used to go into blue chip companies and be on site full-time doing the meals and functions. If there was a kitchen, they would go in and take over the kitchen and do all the cooking for all the employees in the building.

This opportunity was based in one of the major utility companies, whose offices were in the West Midlands. The catering company would take care of all the lunchtime and evening catering requirements for the staff and directors. I remember being invited for an interview and thinking what do I say, because I had no real contract experience in this type of field? I had got catering experience because of the work that I had done in the pub, but the job on offer involved a lot of computer-based work, about which, at this stage, I had no knowledge. I remember going into the interview and she said, "Are you any good with Windows?"

I just blagged it and said "Yes, I can do Windows," not realising what she meant! It was only after I had had the call to say that I had got the job that I began to realise what it involved. I was over the moon and started my new role the following week. After my first few days of bedding in and learning the ropes, my manager said to me that she needed me to type up the following days menu using an existing template and to input the days cash takings including vending machine totals and purchase receipts onto an existing Excel spreadsheet. I realised that I was potentially in trouble! I was thinking 'What do you mean?' but it was at this point that it dawned on me what she meant!

Without blinking an eye, I said to her - she was a lovely lady - "No problem at all, I can crack on with that first thing in the morning." She smiled and thanked me.

The next day, and for the week after, I came into the office at around 6am - our starting time was 8am - and was on the phone to my youngest brother Tom, who was very computer savvy; he guided me through locating and saving files, Excel spreadsheets and word documents etc. Anything to do with computers, Windows, Tom was a fantastic help and got me up and running but, if it wasn't for the fact that I had just blagged this job, I probably would never have got it! Whereas I was expecting to have to clean the office windows, I truly did not know to what she was referring! I was desperate for the job and it opened a new chapter for me, but I did have my brother to thank for all his help, otherwise, I would have might have been out by the end of my first week!

The staff there all liked me – after all, I was a likeable guy - I got on well with everyone, and I made the best of a bad situation by getting in early to learn what I needed to do before they even arrived, so that when they did arrive, I had already had the menu printed up. I could then say, *"This is the menu for today - what do you think of it?"*

"Wow, that's really good, Sean!" my manager would say.

Knowing that I was doing the right thing was a great boost to my confidence. This was my next stage in moving into a Contract Manager's role. I was there for just over two years and I really enjoyed the job, because the hours were a lot better. The catering company worked the same hours as the utility company's employees, unless there was a late-night function or one of the directors needed to entertain. But, normally, it was simply a question of getting there for eight o'clock and leaving around 5pm. It was great – I had the evenings to myself. For me, the sociable hours and the fact that I wasn't going to work feeling afraid or worried, meant that, for the first time, I felt that I had a secure future.

I had left home for the second time around the time that I left the pub trade, and I had now moved into my own digs. This was a one-bedroom flat in Birmingham. I was now 26 and working for a fantastic company with nice people. They didn't sell alcohol on site and there wasn't a bookie nearby. My problems with drink and gambling had arisen previously, mainly because of my proximity to booze and bookies. Once I got away from all that, the problem was no longer there. It was a much quieter lifestyle, it was a normal life, nicer hours, nicer staff and generally a nicer environment to be in. I had talked myself into this job and I was now making my way as one of the managers!

Every job I have had, I have always had romances and I have always enjoyed myself immensely in most jobs that I have had. I have also appreciated these opportunities more since coming out of prison because, locked up in there, you are isolated, you are confined and, in my case with the prison being in Spain, because of language difficulties, you do not always understand what they are talking about! Therefore, when you are out and you have that freedom again, you readjust your values, because you realise what you had lost and what you could have now, so my life changed dramatically. As soon as I came out, I promised myself that I would never ever return to that type of environment but, I am glad that, if ever had to go to prison, it happened when it did as I was able to get it out of my system, while still a young man.

On one occasion I remember, I was in with my boss in our joint office, she was on the phone to her area manager and she was talking to him and I was doing something on my computer and I heard her say '*We can get this on the intranet and get it done asap if you need it today?* Paul, *we also need to include extra functionality on the intranet client portal.*' She said it a couple of times and I paused their conversation midway and she stopped her conversation to her boss and looked over at me, with her hand over the phone receiver. "*It's In-ter-net!*" I mouthed, thinking that I had won a brownie point. She just raised her eyebrows and resumed her conversation, if looks could kill!

Looking back at my social life after I returned from Spain, I have found a girlfriend in every place that I have worked. I think a lot of romances bloom from working together, you have a common connection. When I was working at the pub, I had a girlfriend there who was one of the restaurant staff, and ended up staying on and off at her parents for a while when things were getting bad at home. I was with her for about two years until it ended and then when I was at the contract company, I gradually built up friendships with a lot of the utility company staff as well, and one in particular.

You wouldn't have thought that there could be a better place to work, it was a nice environment, people were great and the hours were good, but I seem to have this tendency, this innate ability to seek out people who appeared to be doing what they were not supposed to be doing. As an example, I went out one night with a few of the kitchen staff, the porters and a few of the chefs – when one of them started rolling a joint, which turned out to be (unknown to me as I had had a few drinks by then) crack and cocaine mixed together. He asked me if I liked it and, as it was making me feel high and giddy, I replied *"Yes, I suppose I do like it!"* I said, *"Am I going to get addicted to it?"*

He replied *"No, just do it in small bursts and you will be fine."*

As a result, I went back on another downward path for about six to nine months, where me and my mate from the kitchens were regularly smoking crack from a bottle in my flat. That's a marked step up in class drugs, from the bit of hash I did in prison. I was living on my own at this stage. I was still at the contract catering company and I had found this guy that I got on well with. He obviously saw me as a crack-head manager with plenty of money and thought that we could indulge in our weekly session by going out to find crack, which was a bit weird.

We would finish work on a Friday, go out for a few drinks and then back to my place, if he was stopping over – I always knew that, if he was stopping over, we would go out on the hunt for crack. He had a dealer contact and he used to phone this guy up and we would go to some back-end street in the base of Birmingham, somewhere where normal people would not go in daylight, let alone at night!

There, we would meet someone who would exchange money for a cling-film wrap of crack that he had in his mouth! At the time we were quite addicted to the idea of smoking the crack without thinking about where it had been. We would then go back to my flat and proceed to smoke it, finding a 1.5 litre coke bottle, stick a hole in the top…you know the rest! We would do this whenever we had funds available.

It was all quite hard and, at the end of about six months, I began to think 'What am I doing? I am blowing one hundred pounds a week on a couple of hours of enjoyment.' When I look back, I am glad that the crack did not become addictive – this type of behaviour is no good and, in fact can kill you or even make you into someone who is zombified. Furthermore, whatever personal characteristics you have, it amplifies them. I am glad that, at the end of those horrendous and ruinous six months, I said *'No, this is silly!'* I couldn't afford to keep burning money like this and, it had to stop and I was able to stop it, probably just in the nick of time. As I mentioned at the start, this a wart's and all type of biography!

I met up with a waitress at the catering company – she was a trolley maid who used to deliver food and drink across all seven floors in the utility company's building. We got on well and we used to enjoy each other's company. I had some good times with her going up and down in the lifts – as you can imagine, we would close the lift, have our merry way together until the lift door opened. It was a bit of fun, it was a bit risqué, but it was a bit of excitement. However, one night I was out with my brother Mike in a local pub when in walked one of the utility company employees I knew from where I worked, she was with her work colleagues and caught my eye and smiled. I went over and started talking to her and we got on quite well. She was a nice lady from a nice family and we kind of clicked.

At the time, I had no money, I'd blown my savings, a lot of it on crack and cocaine and there was no money left in the bank. I hadn't paid my rent in over three months and I was thinking to myself, 'What am I going to do? Where am I going to live?'

I was being evicted the following day by the landlord's company that owned the flat I had been renting, and bailiffs were due in the morning- so I was thinking over and over again, 'What I can do, where can I go?' Then I remembered, the nice young lady I met and chatted to recently in the pub, from the utility company was having a New Year's Eve house party to celebrate the new millennium and she had invited me to come if I was free. Just so happened I was!

So, I went around to her house party. What she was not prepared for or expecting, however, was that I turned up with all my bags! The look of utter surprise then shock on her face was amazing! But fair play to her, she let me in and let me stay the night with a few of the other revellers and we ended up going out together for about two years before we eventually got married. Looking back, I realise that, in every company that I have worked for, I have been able to lock away to one side all that has gone before and move on. I'd have a great time and enjoy it before moving on, this time, however, I was moving on, not on my own, but as a couple!

Chapter 22 – My Best Job

When I left the pub trade, I had kept Joe and Dave's numbers and had kept in contact with them. I never try to come across as desperate in a job interview, even though I might be! That always puts your employer in a better position when he comes to offering you a job with a decent salary. Job interviews are a little bit like playing poker - bluff and keeping your cards close to your chest. I always did my research for any job that I went for, and invariably asked for more than the going rate.

If you sell yourself short, you are not selling yourself properly. If a job salary was £17,000, I would probably ask for £20,000 plus benefits. I always remember someone saying to me "If something is worth having, then it is worth paying for." If I did my research on a position and knew my facts, I would sell myself in that moment. I never did bad interviews but always enjoyed them. No matter how desperate you are in an interview, never come across as desperate and always make them believe that you are the best thing since sliced bread.

My working lives have been a mixture of downs and ups, with the downs meaning sometimes getting involved with people in that environment or being in an environment where it was not safe. In my pub job after coming back from Spain, I was worried about my livelihood and I was getting involved with drink and gambling and I was worried about my safety. In the second job, I was less inclined to drink as there was no alcohol to hand – it wasn't licensed premises, but I was getting involved with worse drugs than I could probably have imagined. However, on the lighter side I had always seemed to meet people who would help me out of that situation – a situation where I thought that I was really going to the depths of despair. I always needed someone to help me get out of those situations. An opportunity always arises, sometimes at the very last possible moment, but it eventually arrives. You always have options.

I was always quite a feeble character really with an additive personality and I needed strong people to help me. I have found that each of the women in my life has always been the stronger person and that's just the way it is! I have learned that I need somebody, obviously female, and they have always been the one that has said *"Sean, you need to get your head back together, sort out your finances, you need to do this that and the other, you need to go and look for a job."*

I suppose that this goes back to the days when I was living at home and it was my mother who was laying down the rules and making me do things. Ever since, I have always relied upon relationships to get me out the mire and to help me. To be honest, every relationship that I have had, I have always enjoyed - I just don't think that the women in my life have always enjoyed it as much as I have!

The role I had at the catering company was one of the nicest and easy going jobs but it wasn't my best job, I loved the staff and the laughs we had but unfortunately the utility company was changing contract suppliers and cutbacks had to be made and I was made redundant from this job, the job I loved. I was out of work yet again and I had blown what money I had. On the plus side I had found and moved in with my girlfriend and things seemed to be going well.

After a few weeks, I was lucky enough to find another job working in insurance, working for a big international insurance company. I joined them as an agency staff member, while working for an employment agency. Getting a new job had not been a major problem because I had previous insurance experience albeit over ten years prior. And as mentioned previously, my criminal record was clean as no searches brought back a hit and so whenever I filled in any job application form, I felt confident to put a tick against the "No" box regarding this. I lied I know but I had to.

I had never lost contact with Joe and Dave after that chance meeting in the pub, despite moving around, as I always spoke to them when my insurance was due. I remember that, one day sometime later, while I was working for the agency, I was working in the insurance company's Claims Department. My car insurance renewal letter came through the post, my policy needed renewing and they always gave me great monthly payment terms to repay my premium, so I was a loyal client. Since you must declare all your changes in occupation, and I was no longer in the hospitality industry. I needed to update my policy. So, I phoned and chatted with Joe to update him.

Joe said, *"What are you doing now mate?"*

"I am in insurance, Joe. I've come full circle here and am working for a major insurance company." At the time, it was a massive company, based in Birmingham. Suddenly, out of the blue, he said *"Why don't you come and work for me?"*

I said, "Joe, *with all due respect, this company is a huge and you are quite a small firm. I might be a small fish in a big pond, but I will learn a lot more."* I didn't tell him that I was working for them as an agency staff member.

"Granted," he said, *"but when you come here, you won't be just a number, you'll be a person that we know and can work with!"*

So, over a matter of a few weeks prior to my renewal we exchanged pleasant conversation about getting me the best renewal price. Then one day, out of the blue, he said *"Look, let me take you out for dinner. Let's go for a curry, Sean."*

So, I went for a nice curry with him and Dave as well.

"As you know Sean, I've now got Dave on board as my Sales Manager and I would like to get you on board too."

I said, *"I don't come cheap, Joe,"* because I never sell myself cheap. *"What salary are we talking about?"* We got down to nuts and bolts over the meal.

Dave said, *"It is worth thinking about moving, Sean, because it will be like the old days at the brokerage in Birmingham. It's just the same sort of office environment."*

"No way Dave! it's never going to be the same."

He said, *"It's really good."*

So, I said slightly warily *"If I come on board Joe, I want something more than just a title. I want to be an owner or a business partner."* I always tried to go in with a high request to test the water. Looking back, I don't think I've ever been for a job interview I didn't get.

"That's my idea as well Sean, I want to have that opportunity as well" said Dave.

Joe turned around and said *"Well I'm thinking of moving to Spain in the next few years. Sean. To be fair, I've been here 15 years and done my fair share of building and developing the company so, therefore, there might be an opportunity for both you and Dave. Who knows?"*

"Are you telling me that I could buy into the business?"

"If you've both got the money at the time when I am ready to offer it, we will take it from there." Joe responded. He always played his cards close to his chest.

At the time, it was just a possibility, but a genuinely potential possibility of buying into the business at some point down the line. So, with that in mind and after talking it over thoroughly with my girlfriend, in 2001, I decided to make the move from a major international insurance company to work for Joe at his much smaller brokers, but with greater potential!

Dave had been head hunted first and had been there about 9 or 10 months. When I started there, I was an Assistant Sales Manager, working with Dave who was the Sales Manager. Then, after I had been there for about two to three years, Dave became Office Manager and I was moved up to Sales Manager.

My job within the company was great, I had some really good times there and I loved day to day office life and the banter that went with the job. I had funny days, too many to recall every situation but there have been some stupid times, some stressful moments and some funny anecdotes.

Then Joe came in and said *"Dave and Sean, can I have a few words with you both upstairs in my office?"* This was suddenly going to become my best job ever!

We went up to his office and he said *"I am going to do what I said I would do when we were in the curry house, and I am moving to Spain early next year. It's something my wife and I have always planned to do. I have set the wheels in motion to sell insurance under the umbrella of this company out there and I am going to live out there permanently, but I want to be sure that the business is going to continue to grow, it is looked after, is well managed and in safe hands. I am therefore offering you two the opportunity to buy into the business. I will sell 48% of the shares and will retain 52% - you will each if you still want them, have 24%."* At the time, a 24% slice of the business, was worth £100,000.

"I am not going to charge you interest on monthly repayments, however to show your interest and commitment I am not going to insist on £50,000 up front" Joe said. *"It will pay my mortgage, paid off in the UK"* he continued – he was a very astute guy and knew that by retaining the 52% he was still the majority shareholder.

Both Dave and I looked at each other and smiled! This was a golden opportunity and one that only comes maybe once in a lifetime. Soon after this brief meeting, both Dave and I became co-owners and directors of the company.

Looking back, I think that Joe had an idea and was trying to recreate our original insurance brokers back from 1986, which had been such a great time and such a wonderful experience. I think he wanted to recreate that team dynamic over again. He was such a nice guy, very worldly wise, very business orientated. He did achieve his aims to a certain degree, because we also located and brought our old friend Pat back into the fold.

At the time, Pat was working for a big commercial company in Birmingham so we got on the phone to him and said, *"Do you want to come and work with us?"* He is such a character with such a great personality. He joined us and it was a great time to regroup the old team. Pat with all his years of commercial experience was responsible for the smooth running and growth of our commercial department, although, to be honest, at that time, we didn't have much of a commercial department. We had Dave, we had Pat, there was Joe and there was me, so we had the core nucleus of the original team that all had got on so well in those long-gone days. It was just the best feeling, the ultimate high getting my foot into the door and becoming a shareholder and becoming an owner of a great business, it felt like I had just bought a large mansion! In 2005 when Dave and I bought into the business, there were only about six staff plus Pat. Over the years, the business has grown and grown, and back in 2018 we had over 30 staff and had to open a second office, so we now have a newer, brasher commercial office.

I remember once, when I was at the contract catering company a few years before, I had the idea of doing a 10 year reunion for all the staff at the insurance brokers at all of ours first job, so I phoned round to those for whom I had a contact number, saying *'Hi it's Sean, remember me? Let's all meet up one night and go out, catch up on old times and enjoy ourselves, do you fancy it?'*

Everyone then rang round to all their own contacts who had worked in the same office so it became a larger number of us, because it was before the days of social media. We had a 10-year reunion evening, which was good. It was one of those nights that you never wanted to end. All the old stories were retold and told again - Do you remember when you handed Sean his name badge, do you remember when Paul set fireworks off just outside that important meeting? What about the time Sean, you got run over running to the bank? We remembered a lot of stuff from those days – we met at 7pm and the time just flew by. We laughed a lot and cried a bit. That was the calibre of the night, time just flew by.

But deep down the real reason that I wanted to do the reunion was that I wanted to meet again that beautiful girl with whom I had had the slow dance all those years ago back in the nightclub. Her name was Lisa. I had a girlfriend

I was living with at the time but I just wanted to meet her, to see her one more time. She was there and I remember I was getting flutters in my stomach. At the end of the night when we were having a curry,

"You know Lisa, I only organised this night so that I could see you again!" I said.

"No, you didn't" she laughed.

"Yes, I did because I had a mad crush on you." I replied.

She just laughed and said, *"You should have just phoned me and asked me out."* She was such a nice person. She was married now, but she was lovely about it. I told her that I had had that soft spot for her. I think that she already knew – I do believe that girls do know when someone has a thing for them.

I remember talking to Joe about her one day in the office, I said to him what a gorgeous person she was both inside and out.

"You didn't know I had a thing once with Lisa?" he said

"You are frigging joking!" I said.

"Yeah, she and I were an item before you even started."

"I never knew that!" I replied. I was so jealous! Joe was always full of surprises.

Chapter 23 – Births, Deaths & Marriages

My first marriage was a marriage of convenience that turned into a disaster. I am sorry but it's true. I was in a relationship with someone who loved me but my love for her was never really reciprocated. I married Jan, my first wife because I was desperate, both financially and emotionally, and I also needed somewhere to live as I was being evicted from my flat. I feel sorry that I let her down so badly as she was a nice, hardworking and honest person who unfortunately met me when I was in a downward spiral. My head was fucked and never really ever in the game.

I should have put more into our relationship but I was just not in the right zone when we were together and our relationship quickly ran its course. She is still the mother of my two oldest children and for that reason I am truly thankful. I would apologise to Jan if I could for being such a rubbish husband but she does not want anything to do with me, which I can understand. She gave birth to my first two children, who I love and adore to pieces.

Looking back, I know now that it was wrong, but I had nowhere else to go and no-one else to turn to and in my moment of chaos and impending eviction I turned to Janet. Consequentially, my first marriage was built on quicksand. We met in 2000 and got married in 2002 and we were together until 2006.

It was a marriage that was never going anywhere. I didn't really bond well with the rest of her family. Initially,

I thought that she was from a privileged background because she was so well spoken but, in fact our backgrounds were quite similar. However, full credit to her, she had worked herself up to a highly responsible position in a major utility company, she was well educated, she was clever, but there was just no affection or love for her on my part at all. We were of a similar age, but we just could not get it all together. Some things are meant to be and some things aren't. I was a fake husband to her and we should never ever have got married. I regret making her life a misery as I was such a shit husband. I just wanted to drink even more to drown it all out and I would come home and open a bottle or two of red wine and just get pissed. She deserved better than me.

I remember that, one day, a colleague from work, Paul, who turned out to be Dave's nephew, asked me to go out to lunch with him. He took me to McDonald's because his sister worked there, and he always got free food. I didn't fancy the food as I was on one of my diets. We walked in and his sister served him. I certainly noticed her and then two weeks later, Dave came up to me and said, *"We need an admin person, Sean, any ideas?"*

I thought for a moment then said, *"What about Pauls' sister? She is working at McDonald's but doesn't want to work there any longer."*

We brought her in for an interview, went through all the proper protocols and she started working for us. I was pleased and we connected straightaway. She was only 17 and I was 38 but we just got on so well. I remember thinking that she was attractive, and she was everything that my wife was not. Her name was Nicki and she was over 20 years my junior and drop dead gorgeous. I was instantly attracted to her, but she had a boyfriend and I was married so, at that time, nothing went any further. She was a great addition to the team and got on well with everyone but every now and then she gave me a smile that melted my heart.

My Grandad had recently passed away and my focus and attention was momentarily distracted. I was extremely saddened by this loss, even though he had reached a ripe old age. My mind was not in the zone at work and I was not switched on really to meetings or dealings with insurance companies. I loved him and he was the last of my grandparents to die. I think in his later years that he had come to see the true me and I believe he eventually became quite proud of me and what I had accomplished. I think I finally earned his seal of approval. I finally may no longer have to carry the heavy weight of being the black sheep of the family!

However, I was looking forward and needed to find a release valve to drown my sorrows following his passing and to toast his life. I remember we had organised a staff Christmas party for our staff and partners. It was quite a messy occasion, with many getting drunk. I remember that Nicki was there with her boyfriend. I had told my wife it was just a party for staff only, as I really didn't want her to dampen my spirits or stop me from having fun.

That night, I saw Nicki and she looked stunning. She was with her boyfriend who, it turned out, she didn't really get on with and, that evening, sent him packing before coming back to my room for a drink. I admit trying to take things further with her as we had a cheeky snog but she was adamant it was not going to go any further, which I respected. After the party, I didn't see Nicki for a few weeks as she had booked a holiday for the New Year so I was counting down the days, all 21 of them until I saw her again.

I was going home to my wife but could not get Nicki out of my mind and was just head over heels. My wife must have realised I was not being myself. I felt so bad as she was five months pregnant at the time with our second child. My world was spiralling again and I was in freefall. I felt such a crappy husband and a schmuck for wanting to cheat on her with Nicki, but the heart does what the heart does!

When Nicki returned to the office in the New Year, she said to me, *"You are my boss and you are married, this is so messed up and wrong!"*

I said, *"Nic, I can't stop thinking about you, I've been counting down the days!"*

"I've been thinking about you too, Sean but you have a pregnant wife!" she replied.

However, we kind of started sending each other text messages and they became increasingly flirtatious, I felt young again and had a smile on my face for the first time since my Grandad died and it just felt right. We got together quite quickly after that, although I was still living with my wife. Then, one day, during yet another heated argument, my wife turned to me and said, *"You know, Sean, we should get a divorce, because you are just not committed to this marriage or interested in me, are you?"*

When she said the word 'Divorce', it was like a red rag to a bull! When she said that, I replied, *"Right Jan, if you want a divorce then I will give you one!"*

I went on to make a big scene and said, *"No, you are God damn right, it's been playing on my mind and it must have playing on yours too, so I think that we should have a divorce. Divorce, if that's what you want then that's what you shall get!"*

Jan was utterly shocked and heartbroken, I felt like this is my one and only opportunity to leave her. I had hurt her badly and was a coward not to confess and be totally honest with her. I made a big scene, went up to the bedroom, took all my clothes out of the wardrobe and put them into the back of the car and drove away, leaving her with my two-year old daughter and another one on the way.

I said, *"I don't care, I'm off as I need some time to think about it."*

I went and stopped in a local Travelodge and told Nic where I was, namely, just around the corner from her. I was there for three months and Nic was coming in and out throughout that period. It was during that time that I, at last, realised that my feelings for Jan had totally diminished. However, I knew that I was in a very bad situation because I was still married, I had responsibilities – one young daughter with another one on the way - as well as the debt I left her in as both Jan and me had re-mortgaged our house to provide the funds for me to buy into the insurance brokerage!

I knew that what I had done was wrong but, on this occasion, my heart totally over-ruled my brain. I knew that I was doing the wrong thing, but I thought to myself, 'Sean you only get one opportunity. I must make a clean break now while the kids are still too young to understand'.

I also knew that if I left it for five or ten years, then I would not be able to do it, as the hurt and pain to the children would be far greater. I was in a totally loveless relationship, so I thought that I had to do it there and then. It seemed to me that this was the right time to make a clean break. If it hadn't happened then, it would have definitely happened at a later stage.

I had a chat with my brother, I said, *"Mikey, I need to have a chat to you."*

He said, *"What's up bro?"*

I said, *"I have left Jan. I don't love her, and I have found somebody else."*

He said, *"No, you can't do that!"* Everyone else that I told, said exactly the same thing.

Mike said, *"You are crazy, at her age, Nic is too young for you, and she might be some kind of gold digger, besides your wife is pregnant!"*

I said, *"You don't know her. I am going to do it as I will never have this opportunity again, I'm never going to find someone as stunning as Nic, so it is going to happen."*

I knew my actions were going to have severe repercussions and cause waves in the family, especially after doing so well and becoming a business owner. But my mind was made up, I knew what I had to do.

Nicki and me then moved in together, we finally left the Travelodge and rented a nice three storey townhouse. This caused great outrage with Jan, who came around to bring some of my remaining stuff and when she saw Nic at the door, she just went absolutely ballistic! She started throwing stuff out of her car, then she brought some boxes out of the boot, made a big scene and upended the boxes in front of me. A lot of things got smashed. You could see the neighbours' curtains twitching and windows opening, lights coming on, for them this was better than an episode of EastEnders!

I said, *"Jan, you have got to go. It's embarrassing"*

"What, embarrassing for you. No, you're the one who is fucking a 17-year old!" she yelled. She was proper shouting at me.

I said, *"I will sign the divorce papers, now just please go."*

I did feel sorry for her, as I knew that she was deeply hurting as it was this chapter in her life that was ending. It was a cruel and devastating breakup of a marriage.

"*No-one in my family has ever divorced, do you understand that?*" she said

I said, "*I don't care, that's no concern of mine.*"

"*I'm humiliated now in the eyes of my family.*" She replied

"*What do you want me to do? I'm sorry but I don't love you!*" I said.

Jan just got in her car and sped off, she was in no state to drive and I felt sorry that I had caused all this to happen, but deep down I knew I had to be cruel to be kind.

Boy did Jan hate me after that! I deserved it and more. However, I know that if I had not made the move then, I would not have the lovely children and the happy marriage that I have now. I had to go through the pain to get out the other side. No-one runs a marathon and expects it to be an easy jog. You go through the pain barrier, both mental and physical. I went through mental torture. At that time, I felt, 'do you know, this might only last six months, it might last a year, but you must go with your heart.'

Nic and I have stuck through it. We have two lovely children together and we are happy, we have been together now for over fourteen years. In December 2011, I took her to New York for a pre-Christmas holiday. We had been picked up by chauffeur from our house and taken to Gatwick airport, where we were taken straight through check-in and customs and given a warm welcome on board by the cabin crew into the first-class lounge. I went down on bended knee and proposed to her at 35,000 feet. The cabin crew knew and when the Captain announced it over the loudspeaker system, there was a huge cheer from all the other passengers when she accepted my proposal, and we were presented with a free bottle of champagne by the Cabin Crew!

In 2012, we decided to get married in New York at midday on the 12th December. There were about 10 of us – We paid for everyone's hotel and we all had a fabulous week there. We had to go through a lot of administration in order to get married in New York and we only got some of the documentation just 24 hours before the ceremony. We had picked New York because we had had such a lovely time there the year before. When we got married, we had our two children with us. It was truly a memorable moment in our lives.

Life is good but like all marriages it has its ups and downs. I went through the mental torture of the breakup of my first marriage but, if I hadn't done it when I did, I honestly believe it would have been worse for my two children from that first marriage. I have a good relationship with Nicki's family. They have never raised any problems over our getting together or the age difference. I am fortunate that my two children from my first marriage and my two from my present marriage get on really well together and have fun times at our house when they stop over. The two boys are of a similar age play on the games console or computer together, while my two daughters, being girls, also get on well, they do dance routines together and do each other's makeup. It works well. My ex has since remarried which I was happy about, so everyone is happy!

Chapter 24–
Alcohol is the Demon Drink

Of all the chapters I have written, this is the one I am the most embarrassed about and I found it by far the hardest to write. I had been a stupid drunk a thousand times before I even met Nicki, but I only really hurt myself. When I got married, alcohol not only hurt me but also my family and writing this chapter was a large bitter horse pill to swallow. It's quite therapeutic now writing it from a clear alcohol-free perspective, at the time of writing I've been sober just over a year and a half, I could not write a cohesive sentence before then, nor could I collect my thoughts and write them down clearly and concisely. Alcohol was turning me into a drooling, selfish vegetable of a human being.

This chapter is specifically dedicated to the demon drink and how I banished alcohol for good. It is a good chapter to read for anyone who is currently suffering from alcohol abuse and hopefully just hopefully you might take something from this and win your personal fight with your inner demons. I really hope you do.

Alcohol was my demon. I hadn't touched "socially acceptable" drugs for over twenty years but the alcohol demon would just not leave me alone, constantly nagging me, it kept whispering, hissing soothing thoughts and eating away at mind, core and self-esteem. I don't know if it was because my mother was an alcoholic and therefore it was passed down in my genes or whether I had one of those addictive personalities where I enjoyed being around people who used to drink a lot and thought it was the "sociable" thing to do like smoking was fashionable to do right up into the late 80's.

On the other hand, for most of my adult life I felt the need and wanted to self-harm myself through drinking to excess. I wanted to feel pain as a way of expiating my sins. I truly felt that through prolonged sessions of heavy drinking and finding the bottom of the bottle was my kind of self-punishment

I will tell you for nothing, alcohol takes but does not give. Alcohol takes your dignity, your respect, your money, your personality and ultimately your family and your soul and gives you nothing in return, apart from a short sad buzz, morning headache and an extra layer of fatty tissue! It's disappointing writing this because over the years the amount of money that I must have spent on alcohol, I could easily have paid off the mortgage on several properties. I gave in to a short-term high in exchange for the potential of a long-term better quality of life. If I ever tell my children anything, it is not to drink or smoke and to save their hard-earned cash.

Alcohol could so easily have sent me right back to that big game of snakes and ladders and it would have laughed at me as I slid all the way down yet another snake - I simply could not see those important ladders. I cannot stress this enough, alcohol is evil. I hate booze now with such hatred like I hate a sex offender or a child killer, I truly do. I cannot say this enough "alcohol is the demon drink!" which we choose to drink freely, it's our choice. It is an attractively packaged poison which is nothing more than decomposing vegetable matter, which can, with a slightly different compound of ethanol, be used by chemical industries to put fuel in your car and to kill bugs.

Alcohol is an anaesthetic, rather than falling into a deep sleep and waking up fully refreshed, you wake up as if from a coma, groggy and drowsy, maybe with a headache just like waking up from an operation.

Now I know a lot of social drinkers who can handle alcohol and they can either take it or leave it and do not drink in the house but only when out with friends. I say good luck to you but my argument is you might be a social drinker but you are still a drinker. You need alcohol to socialise and this chapter probably will not mean that much to you as you can handle your drink. This chapter is mainly for those of us who can't and need alcohol like a crutch to help us through the day.

I don't know whether I was depressed, bored or just enjoyed being the centre of attention when I was buzzing off alcohol. But I know that a quiet voice in the back of my head, that little ego telling me it's OK to drink on my own or to pop into the local newsagents for a couple of miniatures on the way to work, this is not a good voice to have whispering in your ear. It is the Devil luring you in and trying to take advantage of you and your body. The Devil does not have a body of his own so he likes to use yours for his own personal satisfaction and pleasure and he does not give a shit about the condition he leaves you in. Trust me I've been in bad conditions and woken up in some sorry states where I have pissed myself or worse, I have had the sweats and was dehydrated, unable to focus or to navigate my surroundings effectively. If an alien had encountered me as its first contact it would have left shortly afterwards with a dour report on humanity.

I remember the moment when I would describe myself as a functioning alcoholic as I was leaving my family downstairs to say I was going to the toilet and rush upstairs for a few quick swigs of whiskey or a couple of large glugs of red wine from a stash in the bedroom wardrobe. I thought this will be fine, you will go downstairs and all will be exactly the same apart from one thing I had to nod or smile because if I opened my mouth to talk the game would be up, I would be a little bit slurry and my wife Nic would sense something was not right.

I was just acting in the character of a happy family guy but I wasn't. I was feeling drained and depressed and I didn't know why I was. I was comfortably well off, we had a nice house and my business was doing well, I had my loving and beautiful wife Nic and four adorable children who I loved so much. Why was I depressed? Was I bored? I do not know but I know one thing I was addicted to alcohol. Have you ever woken up at 4am when the house is dark and quiet to sneak into the wardrobe for a quick hit of whiskey? I have! Have you ever gone to your car under the pretext of getting something, opening the boot and swigging from a miniature Jack Daniels bottle? I have!

The number of bad things I have done while drunk are just disgraceful and writing these down in black and white now for the first time is just so embarrassing. I feel ashamed of myself.

There was the time I borrowed my friends Porsche Panamera to impress my family gathering the following day. My wife was away with her sister in Tunisia. On the morning of the family Mass, I got drunk (whiskey was my chosen poison at this time). I then drove with my two little children who were aged about four and one, on an eighty-mile round trip, totally drunk. I called my wife to tell her I was drunk in a super car about 40 miles away from our home. She ran up a £500 phone bill on her Pay-As-You-Go mobile from Tunisia phoning me multiple times, then calling her family to come and collect our children. That was just a total embarrassment and humiliation.

On another occasion I treated my wife and her sister to a day trip to London and while they were away, I took my kids to our local tennis club. While the children were playing in the play area, I got drunk. It was only about 10.30am and I was the first to get served alcohol at the bar. My son Will fell while playing in the soft play area, he was crying his little heart out but I just thought he had sprained his arm. My wife called home and Will answered the phone crying and told his Mom that I was fast asleep. She rushed back on the train with her sister, missing out on her well-deserved break to take our son to A&E. I was an absolute disgrace and they confirmed to my wife our son had a hairline fracture in his left arm.

I became quite good at masking just how drunk I was. On holiday, I was pissed and after a lovely meal in a nice restaurant in Ibiza (I could remember none of the meal), while my wife was taking our son down some stairs. I followed and put my two-year old daughter on my shoulders and proceeded to stagger down four of five steps exiting the restaurant and fell ass over tit onto the floor with my little girl falling as well. Luckily my daughter, Rose was fine but my wife was so angry and mad at me for being so stupid when I was obviously so drunk.

One other time, my wife was at work and I went to pick up our children from school. I called her to say our son, Will was complaining he couldn't see properly out of his eyes, he hadn't said anything to the teachers and waited to tell me.

"What do you MEAN he can't see?" She screamed at me on the mobile "Let me speak with him!"

After talking with our son Will, she spoke to me and said "I'm in work, take him to A&E right away!"

"I can't…" I replied

"What do you mean you can't take our son …?" There was a pregnant pause as the penny dropped.

"ARE YOU DRUNK?" she shouted.

My silence was all the acknowledgement she needed to realise once again I was about to be a massive fucking let down! I had been drinking whiskey in a local pub before picking up our kids from school, I thought it was going to be an easy and straight forward school pick up. She panicked and immediately dropped everything and left work early to take him to A&E and spent another very anxious evening there while I was passed out at home with our daughter Rose. Nic came back from A&E exhausted and anxious to find I had been sick in our son's bed while our daughter had been asleep upstairs. I can only say that my utter reliance towards alcohol blinkered everything else. That little voice in my head kept saying that everything will be ok and fine if you have another sip of whiskey. I was an idiot and cannot believe how I was and it makes me feel like the scum of the earth. After hospital tests my wife was told our son may need glasses as he was suffering from excessive eye strain from schooling and sports. I was only informed the following day by my wife after I had sobered up. She was obviously extremely angry with me, having stayed awake with our son all night and cleaning the sick stained bed sheets which I had left her.

I also went on a lad's holiday for James, a very good work colleague's, 21st birthday, and he's a great guy. There were four of us heading to Las Vegas for a long weekend, including my business partner Dave. I was a total drunk from the start of the holiday until the finish and I know this grated heavily with Dave as I was just acting like a drunk all the time. I embarrassed myself by drinking heavily and prior to coming back on the plane, Dave said "Guys, we've all had a great time, drank plenty but we need to stop now or else we won't be able to get on the plane!".

He was looking mainly at me. With that said, I turned around to the bar tender, raised two fingers and ordered two large Bloody Marys, both of which I drank in quick succession, all drinks in the casinos are free! I was paralytic drunk at the airport and Dave was pissed off with me, he was worried I was not going to get on the plane and would potentially be a liability for everyone.

We all went to a fast food chain inside the airport to try and sober me up and there were no tables free apart from just the one which just had loads of leftover crap and rubbish on it, none of the lad's wanted to move the rubbish as it was so busy, I just went straight over to the table with my burger and drink and with one large sweeping hand movement, launched the whole litter and drinks on to the floor. Everyone in the place just stopped and stared at me as I proceeded to sit down and consume my food, unaware of the carnage I had just caused. Dave just looked at me in disgust and walked off seething. I was a drunk and I didn't care who I upset nor did I have a way of controlling my drinking. I was the ultimate loose cannon! And it is with no surprise that I have never ever been invited ever again on a lad's holiday or even a works night out with anyone that knows me well. I wonder why?

Back at home, I was totally ignorant of my family's feelings and did not give a damn as long as I had alcohol. That's how bad I was and I was despicable and feel so lucky and happy now to have got rid of my demons. Even though I thought I had my demons under control, I was on a slippery hell slide to oblivion and only I could help me! I was hiding alcohol just like my mom and I was out of control just like her as well. I was a true definition of an alcoholic, borderline even a functioning one!

The list of my intoxicating experiences goes on and on there are countless more episodes which I could write about but I believe you can get the flavour of my selfishness and my total lack of caring and disregard to the ones I loved because I felt alcohol was more important, it had a grip over me which I could not control. I used to drink and drive all the time and not just a little over the limit, I would be two or three times over. I was a total disgrace and thank God I never killed anyone while I was driving. I am ashamed of the person I had become; alcohol was king and my family was just nothing.

Any other wife in her right mind would have left me for dust but Nic was different. She saw something in me I did not even see in myself. I think she knew deep down I was a decent person and I think she felt our marriage and family was worth saving. I knew I had to change or I would lose everything. I had it all but I did not want to give anyone the satisfaction of laughing at my demise. I did not want to ruin my family life and most of all I did not want to lose my children, all this was a worry for me when I was sober. When I was sober, I would get really depressed that I was losing everything I held dear and loved and that made me want to drink. It was a downward spiral.

My drinking had been going on for years and the moment I had it all I just wanted to get wasted. I was obviously not well and needed help but I didn't ask for help from anyone. I didn't go to a doctor or a hypnotherapist or anyone counsellor, I knew this was my problem and I knew I had to sort out my shit.

Every day I would wake up and my first thought was always the same, when can I have a drink today, when can I have a sly drink without anyone noticing. My hissing demon voice would tell me know will know you've had a cheeky sip Sean, you will be fine, trust me! I was a stupid drunk. I used work as a means to try and take my mind off alcohol. Work helped but it was just a band aid over a deep wound. I was just letting alcohol hurt me, I was in a downward spiral and alcohol was my way of self-harming. I wanted to feel the hurt and pain that I knew I would get from drinking alcohol and getting to the bottom of a whiskey bottle as soon as possible was my solution, my remedy to the addictive and ongoing requirement for booze I had inside of me. Alcohol, Sleeping and Eating were the Holy Trinity and nothing else mattered. Maybe I felt guilty for being such a bad husband and father, maybe I felt bad for all the shit I had caused people over the years, I was just so deeply depressed.

Then like everything in my life, things happened. One day as I was in a bleak moment of despair. I was upstairs on my bed sitting on the side of it half-dressed with my hands holding my head resting forwards. I was wondering what the hell I was doing with my life, whether to kill myself or just have another drink, my son Will walked into the room and must have been watching me for a moment or two.

He must have been about eight at the time and we have a thing called a "Daddy Deal". If I ask him if he has done something wrong and he hasn't he will say to me *"Daddy Deal I haven't"* and I know straight away that he is telling me the truth. My son has never ever broken a "Daddy Deal" and we both hold those two simple words sacred; it is a sacred trust and unshakeable bond I have with my son and it works. It has worked for us since he was a small boy and it had never been broken. Any way he walked over to me, stood in front of me and said *"Dad I will make you a Daddy Deal. I will get up for school every morning without a problem and wash, brush my teeth and get dressed all by myself, if you stop drinking?"*

He then extended his little finger on his right hand, his deal finger to me. I stared at his little finger for about ten seconds, I knew if I did not cross his little finger with mine he would never trust me again and probably not want to cross my finger in the future and if I did cross his finger, the deal would be cemented. I needed something to happen and this was that moment. After about a minute I crossed his little finger and he smiled, such a beaming smile that I remember it still. I heard him running down the stairs and telling his mom his good news and I knew he felt so proud. I had committed to an unbreakable bond, a trust I held sacred with my son. I also felt like a boat with an oar, I had direction and a path and alcohol was the rocks and heavy waves to avoid.

I was in total denial and I thought our marriage was fine, I knew I had an alcohol problem but I did not realise just how close it was to all just falling apart, until I had a long frank heart-to-heart conversation with my wife and she said she was on the verge of leaving me as she could not cope with me drinking anymore. She knew I had a problem and had previously tried to help me but she had our children to consider and prioritise. I was becoming a dead weight. I told her about my deal with Will and that this time I really desperately wanted to give up and I could not go back on a Daddy Deal! I was tired of alcohol and I was just killing myself slowly by poison. I truly felt the difference now was that I wanted to change from the core of myself, I wanted to change for the better. I really and truly believe the switch got flicked!

Now I had to do something to kick this demon out of my life forever, I needed to kick the habit. The secret of kicking alcohol for me was this I started small, I changed one small thing in my life I thought could be easily changed. Every small change was a small win. When I got a small win, it gave me a mental boost, a small victory. Start small with just one insignificant thing that you can control easily. I started by listening to music and podcasts.

I knew I could not talk or converse properly as my brain nerve endings were fucked after years of abuse but I did enjoy listening to a good podcast. I thought to myself if I'm listening to podcasts then I'm not drinking. I needed to do anything to take my mind off alcohol, it was small steps, very small baby steps.

I started with meditation, in a quiet space with some peaceful background music, then this moved on to meditating then listening to podcasts, to reading historical fiction, to walking the dog whilst listening to some tunes and books, then to jogging around the block with my headphones, to going to the gym. Gradually, I built on those baby steps and slowly but surely, I began to take the alcohol out of the equation altogether by replacing it with things that I liked to do or that made me feel better, making my body and mind feel better was key to my recovery. I was nearly four stone overweight when I last drank alcohol. I needed to start living healthy, my body was fucked and my brain had little or no capacity to function, those neurons were just not firing. After a couple of months after giving up booze I was hitting the gym hard and meeting new like-minded friends at the gym. My new circle of gym friends was growing and then I met a gym buddy called Mez who would be my rock and my go to guy for whenever we were both at the gym. I think its important to have a gym friend to help you and motivate as results come quicker, I was so pleased to meet Mez, such a lovely and friendly guy. We instantly clicked and have since become very close friends. I also met a fantastic personal coach who is a part time semi-professional football player and part time babe magnet, called Darryl. He helped me lose just over three stone in under 18 months. It was a strict food and exercise regime and he motivated me all the way. After 18 months of losing the weight, I felt fantastic, my body looked in the best shape and my self-esteem was back to an all-time high. About a dozen of us from the gym including Mez & Darryl entered and took part in a gruelling 10km Tough-Mudder assault course which I could never have done previously, we completed it in a respectable 3 hours. Darryl has since become very good friend and mentor.

Giving up alcohol is a day-by-day progression. For me, it was literally a moment by moment thing but by breaking a routine and filling that routine with something more productive and rewarding, you eventually have after a short period of time that "flick that switch" moment and alcohol no longer has the same hold over you as it did before. Trust me when I say at some point in quitting alcohol if you try, you will come to that "switch moment". Break your routine and substitute alcohol for something that interests you. Start small and slowly but surely alcohol will get demoted and ultimately will get shut out from your mind, trust me it will work if you give it a try, but remember baby steps.

I do not condone other people for social drinking, they may be able to walk away from alcohol the next day, however I doubt they can give up alcohol totally. I however could not and will never ever want to feel the effects of alcohol ever again, I absolutely hate it with a passion, my mind and body are now thankfully working in perfect harmony. I do still have down days where I am feeling a little bit low but I have pushed alcohol so far away that its now well outside and firmly quarantined. I don't experience the extreme highs and lows of depression that I previously did when I was drinking. I never ever hear that whispering voice and I feel a whole lot happier and fitter! You can do it, I know you can, just remember baby steps and small changes leading to bigger ones.

I truly hope that one day you might be able to write to me and say "Sean, I flicked that switch!"

Chapter 25 – Reflections and Thoughts

Sometimes opportunity knocks and you are just not ready, it might just not be your moment. For instance a few years ago I completed an online audition request to go on a popular family game show, I probably shouldn't mention the name of the show for legal reasons but it was hosted by Bradley Walsh. I completed the forms and forgot all about it. About six months after completing the form, I got a call from the show's producer asking if we were still interested in taking part and whether we would be able to do a General Knowledge quiz over the phone with a couple of the family members. Of course, we said yes and did the phone quiz and were pleased when we were told we had passed and were through to the next stage of the audition process. We were all excited and a few days later I got a telephone call from a show executive asking if we could all meet up for a group day where they were auditioning other families. They obviously wanted to see us and maybe to see if we were television material, did we present well and were we what they were looking for. It was an interview process but instead of a job it was for a chance to go on the telly. We were all nervously excited about going and secretly I was hoping that if nothing else we might bump into Bradley. On the day of the show audition, I had had a few drinks to calm my nerves and all of us went along to a nice hotel which had pre-booked a large room to do its second round of auditions. We waited patiently for our turn and when we were called into the room, the producers and the some of the shows staff were in the room dancing around to some music and having fun,

"Let's dance to this tune guys!" someone shouted.

My family and me just sat straight down in some front row seats and watched bewildered as they danced around singing. I honestly did not know what was going on and we just looked at each other as if we had walked into a wrong room where a group were doing their local theatre production rehearsals.

With hindsight we should have realised it was all part of the audition process to see if we would join in. Maybe if I had had a few more beers inside of me then I might of jumped up and danced, or maybe if I had not drank at all I would have done better. It did not come as a surprise that after our stony faced silence at the beginning and me messing up a few questions when they played a game with us that our luck had finally ran its course and we were not offered a place at the final auditions, where no doubt Bradley would definitely have made an appearance. It's probably for the best that we did not get through as I had lied on the application form anyway regarding my history, I hadn't expected us to get this far to be fair. I was just gutted I had let the rest of the family down as I was not on my game and was slightly drunk.

Looking back over my life so far, there have been many changes of direction in terms of where I was living and where I was working. At all stages along that journey, the decisions that I have made have largely been influenced both by people with whom I was in contact – family and work colleagues – as well as by location. Some of the decisions that I have taken have proved to be correct while others have been well, shit! It's all a life learning curve.

Years ago, while drinking in a pub with some friends, we couldn't find a local taxi to take us home - we had a lightbulb moment! I had helped design, create and get a reputable software team to build us an App. I always enjoyed the buzz of doing something new and exciting. We each invested thousands of pounds (and hours) in a business venture that we all thought would be the next big thing. Our great idea – was to get customers to use our taxi app; which would automatically request several local taxi firms (within a certain radius of the client) to place an instant bid on a potential job. Based on the clients journey, destination, number of passengers etc, the taxi firm input a 'price and time' via our app and the customer if they needed one straight away, could then choose either the 'best-reviewed' taxi firm, the one arriving the 'quickest' or just 'cheapest' one.

It had great potential but we needed a large venture capitalist to come on board, plus we needed to sign up hundreds of taxi firms. This was before the time of the taxi apps that are around today. Great idea, but we just needed a huge injection of cash. It could have worked, but upon reflection we just didn't have the resources or cash to take it to the next level. Right idea, wrong time!

My Mom, oh wow, I could have written a whole chapter on my mother! My relationship with her was always difficult and traumatic, fraught with arguments and then making up. It really was the reason that I left home and began my adventure, I never felt that she loved me and in return, I never knew how to love her, not until we both grew a lot older and wiser. She died suddenly and alone which I found hard to deal with at the time but we had made up. When I visited her in her final years, we truly had some heartfelt and tender moments. My Mom got much better over time and boy, she loved all her grandchildren immensely and had strangely become very similar to my Nan, the Nan I had and remembered so fondly growing up, back in Alum Rock. It was our continuous battle of wills over the first years of my life that led me, firstly, to attempt suicide and secondly to me leaving home in search of the gold on the streets of London. Chance meetings there took me to Brussels and thence to Alicante where, in moments of madness, I first attempted to defraud a bank and then to rob one!

These were harrowing times, as I have described in the book but, I honestly believe that, in the end, they straightened me out and, more importantly, strengthened my character. However, as I now describe, when I returned from Spain at the age of 24, it was the way that my family, including my Mother, put their arms round my shoulders and opened the door on a new life at home, a situation that was further strengthened by returning to work with Joe and Dave, who completed the transformation, all of them together creating a "Road to Damascus" moment that offered me just one great opportunity to transform my life. In this final chapter, you will see how and why this worked and how, as a direct consequence of their love and support, I became the man that I am today.

The opportunity was created by my Father and two brothers tracking me down and then making the effort to come and visit me in prison. When I was called to the Visitor Section, I could not imagine who could be visiting me as I had told no-one where I was. When I saw Dad and my two brothers through the glass window, it was like a spiritual awakening because, initially, I was worried as to whether or not they would accept me and forgive me for all that I had done wrong and all the hurt that I had caused to all my family and friends. However, when I saw the look on their faces and the love in their eyes, there was just so much love coming through that glass panel it made me realise that there was much more to life than where I had been for the last five years.

When I was in prison and my fellow inmates became aware that I was leaving, I was made all sorts of offers - that they needed someone on the outside, a drugs mule or someone who could work on the drugs boat for them and many more tempting but unlawful offers. All of them were couched in the terms of *"See what you can do to make a wedge of cash to stash until you are back in here with us!"*

These offers were being made to me and, I must confess that, at that stage, I was faced with the dilemma as I had no idea what I was going to do when I left prison. Could I make a go of it on my own or was I now consigned to a life of crime, drugs, alcoholism and retribution? To be honest at that stage, sitting in our cell or while wandering around the yard, I just did not know which way I would turn. Was I strong enough mentally to make the readjustments? What would I find if I managed to make it back to England? Would my family reject me? Would I be able to get a job and, if so, what sort of job could I expect?

Throughout the compulsory flight home to England, I was alone on the plane among a group of passengers who were wondering throughout the flight just who they had got in their midst! However, on that day in 1994 at Gatwick Arrivals, when I got off the plane and made my way, slowly and uncertainly though passport control and customs – I didn't have any luggage, just what I stood up in to my utter amazement I saw my family with their arms outstretched towards me and big smiles on their faces, I knew that the decision had been made for me. I just knew that I had a home to go to when I got back. I knew that when I left prison and went back to the UK, there would be a home there. Before, I did not know whether I would be welcome or not, especially because of the relationship with my Mom.

Throughout the journey by car back to the West Midlands, Dad and my two brothers kept emphasising that Mom had changed, that she was now on tablets and was in a far better frame of mind than when I left over five years ago – was it really only five years, it all seemed much longer and I had experienced so much. I just kept saying that *'Yes, but she's probably changed because I have not been in the life for the last five years!'*

I did feel that by them turning up and extending the olive branch, I knew then that my decision was made as to which way I was going to go - I could go one way or the other when I left prison and I knew that I did not want to go back to prison.

It was an enormous comfort blanket to know that I still had the support and love of my family. This was so, so crucial for me as I had never felt a lot of love in my life up to that day. In fairness, I didn't feel that I was deserving of any love and I did not know how to love. I was totally removed from it. My relationship with my two brothers was the only true love that I had had – we had grown up together, we knew each other's strengths and weaknesses – and when I saw Mikey and Tom through that window, the feeling of love just came straight through to me, it was very emotional and I have to admit that I did well up!

When I came out, I knew that I wanted to make my life better. I did not want to go back to being just a "bum", I did not want to go back down that route of being involved in drugs, I didn't want any more trouble with the police. I'd been there and done that and now it was time to make a new way through life. Upon reflection, I was glad that it had happened at that time in my life because, as I have already said, I truly believe that if it had happened later, it would have been far more catastrophic. It had given me a taste of what I did not want to happen and had created a longing for a better life. I was still young – nearly 25 – and I had been given the chance to carve out a completely new life.

The next major turning point was that fortuitous meeting up for a second time with Joe and Dave. I was working in the pub and they just happened to walk in, not aware that I was working there, and the look of sheer amazement mixed with bewilderment on all our faces made us all just stand and stare open mouthed. Over the next few weeks, we met up on several occasions and I made no secret of where and what I had being doing over the previous five years, what I had done and my time in jail. Both Joe and Dave could look beyond this and see the person inside me and they had known me from our previous working relationship in the past and under the right circumstances and with the right amount of love and support, I could turn myself round. After all, everyone deserves a second chance.

However, Joe made the offer of employment to me and, while at that time, I was working for a major international insurance company and Joe's operation was a lot smaller in comparison, from what he and Dave told me, I quickly realised that this could be the golden opportunity, with the potential of buying into the business I was looking for, and maybe just maybe to make my first million! Mind you, I was also aware that if I screwed up, then I would be back on the scrap heap big time! However, the last five years had convinced me that there was no way that I was going to make a mess of it!

Therefore, when I had the opportunity to invest in the business, I grasped it with both hands. When opportunity came knocking, I did not shirk the chance. I knew that if I ever gave Joe the impression that I was unsure and was wavering as to whether I wanted to take the opportunity, there was another guy in the office, Neil, who had worked in the business longer and he was the office manager. He and Joe got on well, he had been there for about 5 years before I joined, and it was only because I had known Joe when we were both at Auto Insurance in Birmingham that he offered the opportunity to me. However, I knew that if I had wavered or if he had looked into my eyes and thought that I was not 100% committed, then I knew he would have offered it to Neil. Joe and Dave were both big football supporters and they both had their own season tickets. I also knew that Joe would have got on just as well with Neil as he did with me. I knew that this was my one and only chance of reprising my future. This was the opportunity that I had been waiting for and asking Joe for.

I honestly believe that people who know me, know that I am not inherently a bad person. I had always thought of myself as a bad apple, but they saw more in me than that and had recognised the real me. There is no nastiness or any malicious side to my nature, no matter what has happened to me and no matter how I have been treated, either by members of my family or by people in general.

When Joe did make the offer to me to buy into the company, I said, *"Yes of course but I just need to have access to the last few years' accounts"*

"Yes, that's fine. Take the accounts and come back to me when you have made your decision."

I knew if I did not take this opportunity, Joe was going to Spain in any case and he would simply have offered it to

Neil. I literally put all my eggs in one basket. I had left a major international insurance company to come and work with him in a very small brokerage with only about six or seven staff – it's now over 30. At the time, I could see a great potential for the business.

When he did offer it to me, it just felt as though all my prayers had been answered – I just knew that this was the winning lottery ticket that I had been waiting for. At this stage, I was the Assistant Sales Manager and Dave was the Sales Manager, Neil was the Office Manager and looked after the whole of the office, Dave looked after the sales department and I was Dave's junior. When Joe handed the business in the UK over to us, it was all handled formally. We became co-owners and directors, each holding 24% of the shares with Joe holding the other 52%. Dave and I worked to each other's strengths – I took on human resources, salaries, payroll, claims and personal insurances while Dave concentrated on building up the commercial business. In all honesty, I really did have to hang on to Dave's shirt tails because once he was a co-owner, he had fantastic innovative ideas and was dynamic in driving the business forwards, I could only hope I could keep up with him.

Dave, to his credit, spotted a niche in the market that had not been fully exploited and was not being promoted, and that was motor trader and SME commercial insurance. The larger commercial brokers turn up their nose at anything under £5,000 in premiums but for us this was major business that could give us perhaps a £1,000 commission from the insurance companies. Dave is very good at building solid ties with the insurance companies whereas it was not one of my strengths. He would take them out and get to know them on a one-to-one basis, so that whenever we had a one to one meeting, we would brainstorm and say what is going to be the next big thing.

Back in 2005, nobody was touching the motor trade, so Dave went to the insurance companies and said that we wanted to do bespoke motor trade scheme. Their response was *"What do you mean, motor trade?"*

They had dealt with the vehicle companies and the large dealers but no-one had seriously looked at the small part time traders, not just the actual dealers but it might just be someone who wanted to sell a few cars off his drive, or maybe a mobile mechanic who wanted insurance so that he could collect a car and take it to his workshop, to an MOT station or to get some parts for it.

Dave quickly reached agreement with an insurance company with whom he got on well and it just took off to such an extent that we had to open a second office and take on more staff to handle the enquiries. We decided that this was the way forward and started to get a good name for ourselves in this field of insurance. Today we have one office in Dudley and one in the City centre. We decided that one office would be more upmarket so that we could take our commercial customers there. Pat, from our previous time, came to work with us for a few years but, when I became a director and ultimately his boss, our relationship changed, and he moved on.

This was an opportunity that I did not want to miss, and I knew that if we developed a good rapport with the insurance companies, then this business would become a real money spinner. Joe had not been into commercial insurance in a big way, he was more interested in smaller policies, such as motor bikes, as he was keen on motorbikes, whereas Dave and I could see a much bigger picture.

The premiums that we were talking about were like manna from heaven for the insurance companies because the type of customer that we targeted offered a low claims ratio to premiums collected, most motor traders fix their own damaged vehicles or have connections in the trade who can help, so we tended not to hear from them until it was time to renew. The insurance companies were very happy and we were building not only the business but also making excellent connections with the insurers. If they see you giving them a profitable book of business, they are more likely to assist you with other schemes. Joe was happy, he had gone off to Spain where he was developing his own business and had great results coming through from us back in the UK.

Dave and I worked together well. If I went up to him and just said such and such is a good way forward, he would reject it immediately but if, on the other hand, I was to go in and say, this is an idea as to how we can open up a new niche market, I have done the research and there are only three or four brokers currently doing it but they are not taking it seriously despite the fact that it could be potentially a larger profitable market, he would listen, think it through and, once we agreed it had wheels, then it was all systems go. There is no such thing as a bad idea. We also tied up with a reputable finance company so that we could offer the clients a finance package, bearing in mind that some of these premiums could be over £2,000 and most people do not want to lay that out in one hit. Dave got on really well with the representative of the finance company and got us some really good deals that offered great finance packages to our clients. Happy clients were always good business.

We knew what policies we were going for, particularly the low hanging fruit that other brokers weren't bothered about; we were able to offer a good finance rate but this was only because we had the right connections with the insurance and finance companies and that really drove the business forward. Brokerage for us was all about providing a great policy and service at a competitive premium that provided a good deal for the client and for us. We now have our own in-house lead generating team in our commercial office, working for us and they generate a lot of business by targeting very specific market sectors through very strategically developed campaigns. We give them very specific instructions because we know what business we can sign on and they bring in the leads to match our precise criteria. At the end of the day there is no point trying to sell adult shoes to a toddler!

I have made my share of good money now to the point where at the age of forty-nine, I have retired from the insurance company I co-owned and remain only a shareholder in the business. I earned a very competitive salary and dividend and have been fortunate enough to have also invested in property and a few years ago I also took some sage advice from a good friend of mine who was a hedge fund manager. This portfolio of investments together with my shareholder dividends has ensured my family and myself are now financially secure for life. I live a comfortable but not overly lavish lifestyle. I don't regret anything because if one thing hadn't happened in that precise order at that exact time then I probably wouldn't be writing this book right now.

I have lived a very full life and over the past thirty years I've easily spent around a small fortune on drink, gambling, drugs and a few unprofitable business ventures! I turned 50 years old in 2019 and I'm sure there is still much more life and adventure to come! I have drunk far too much and taken far too many drugs and, as a result, I think that my brain cells have slowed down to the point where most are either on strike or simply don't give a crap! I suppose, with Karma, I haven't looked after them so why should they look after me? I have lost count of the times over the years that I have been in a conversation with someone and just frozen or my words have just come out like those of a four-year old. I really hate small talk with a passion and, if I can avoid it, I will. The countless number of times in the past that I have started a conversation or been involved in a conversation with absolutely nothing plausible, relevant or interesting to say and simply say things like "Do you remember...?" or "What was I going to say ...?" or "Do you know what..?" I just look at the person that I was talking to and am filled with pity – that's what having a braincell workforce on strike does to your self-esteem and intelligent conversation. So, don't drink, smoke or take drugs and enjoy a great life – job done! Over the last couple of years in an attempt to reinvigorate my brain cells I've given up alcohol and done a lot more reading which I enjoy immensely.

I've now learned to abide by a brief set of rules, a worthwhile set of self-help rules that have helped me over the last few years. They have been a good focal point – not rocket science - but they have given me help in reaching my maturity, albeit somewhat delayed, and they have helped shape me into the person I am today. I am not saying that they are a strict set of rules, but they are "my life guidelines;" do with them as you feel fit. They are not your run of the mill rules, like - don't drink, don't smoke, don't do drugs or gamble but they work for me and that's all I can say. At the end of the day you have to live life to the fullest and experience as much as possible, as I said at the beginning of my book, I never wanted to be a hermit. Over the years, I must be honest, I have broken most of them but, for me, they are there as my guidelines, make up your own if you want. They are in no particular order of importance:

1. Be ready. You will have setbacks in life, accept that as a no brainer, a done deal but when opportunity finally knocks and it will, make sure you are ready - how many times have we all looked back and realised that, if we had made a different choice, our lives might have been totally different – that well-known phrase "hindsight is a precise science!" all too often rings increasingly true. When I had left home, I thought that the streets of London were paved with gold and the opportunities would be bountiful and open up for me. In fact, the only opportunity that opened up for me was that 6-foot long filing cabinet! How wrong could I have been! Similarly, when I went to Brussels and then to Spain, I again thought that the world was my oyster, only to find that the oyster shell had closed tightly on me and I was in jail for robbing a bank! On the occasion when I was finally offered a wonderful opportunity to invest in the insurance brokerage, I definitely made the right choice but, I'm just thankful I did grab it with both hands!

2. Do your own research and obtain reviews on everything - This applies no matter whether it's a business venture, an interview or even a holiday – do your research! Remember, no-one owns all the rights to being brilliant! The internet has all the answers to all your questions and you would be a fool not to use it. I literally use Google for everything and would not make a commitment without first checking reviews first and foremost and doing my own online research.

3. Try saying "Yes" more times than you say "No"- I firmly believe in positivity. I also think saying "Yes" opens more doors than saying "No". This might seem obvious. However, over the years I have found that sometimes coming out of my comfort circle and agreeing to something and saying Yes has created some of my greatest and fondest memories. I have walked across a stretch of the Sahara for my late mom for charity when I said yes. I have joined gyms and become members of chess and clubs which I would not have done in the past because I said yes. Saying Yes more often than No was tough at first but I can honestly assure you from my own personal experience it's definitely worked out in a beneficial way. I have made a whole new wonderful circle friends by saying Yes. I have even found that responding positively to some spam emails has given me some fun as well, albeit I wouldn't recommend this to everyone!

4. Get a good night's sleep, at least seven hours - In my humble opinion, this is a sound maxim and is even better if you wake up to a pint of water; your body has been left dehydrated for several hours, so fill the tank. You cannot perform to your maximum potential if you are not fully awake and up to speed. Sleep is the elixir of life and helps your body repair and much more. Just type into Google the benefits of a good night's sleep and you will see the multitude of positive bullet points, including reducing stress, increasing memory and helps lose weight amongst many, many other benefits.

5. Forgive your own mistakes - Learn to forgive but not forget your mistakes, they are already history. Dwelling on a mistake does nothing for your mental wellbeing. Move on and look forward even to making more mistakes, if you're making mistakes at least you're still alive and you can learn from them. Just try not to make the same mistake twice. I have made some howlers in the past but I'm only human and besides, anyone who hasn't made a mistake hasn't lived.

6. Be your own hero – Do something nice, anything really. Be the best version of yourself! One good deed improves your mental well-being and may even go some small way to counter any bad mistakes you have already made. Whenever I take my dog, Buster out for a walk I always bring a large plastic bag with me to collect plastic bottles on the ground, I hate litter anyway with a passion so this gives me exercise and a way of doing a bit of litter clearance. It is great for your karma which I believe is ever present. I'm not going to dwell on this one too much, but if you want some positive energy just try it, you will feel a lot better about being you.

7. Take time out - This is one of my personal favourites, life is travelling past us at a furious pace and sometimes it's worth just stopping to take account of where you are and what you have got. Do this in private on your own when no-one else is around as its better to think your best thoughts in your own privacy. I like to leave my phone in the house and when I take my dog for a walk, I sit on a bench and just chill. I think of five things I really and truly appreciate in my life (non-materialistic) and even meditate sometimes, which I find really cleansing to my body, mind and spirit.

8. Give loose change to the homeless - They need it more than you do. It is all too easy to simply look down upon a man or a woman who is down on their luck and to pass judgement as to whose fault it is that they are where they are and to assume that they are simply drug addicts and/or alcoholics. They may well be drinking and taking drugs but, in a great many cases, there is a genuine reason why they are where they are.

Talk to them, not at them, have a conversation, they are human beings and deserve respect. I know from my own experience just how easy it is to slip into this way of life but equally just how much harder it is to get out of it. Furthermore, modern society is all too quick to pass judgement while not enough is being done to help those caught in this trap.

In the years since I was reduced to sleeping in a filing cabinet, in doorways or under bridges, much has been done to try to move towards these unfortunate people and to offer help and assistance and a path to reintroduce them back into society. In some cases, this may simply be a hostel where you can go for a night's sleep, a bath, wash your clothes and have a meal while, in others, it may involve a much longer programme aimed at getting the person off the street completely.

Sadly, the amount of help varies from town to town and from country to country, as I found on my travels, but, all too often, it is limited simply by the amount of money (government or donations) that is available. I know from talking to the homeless that most have slipped down the ladder and through the crack, often through no fault of their own and ended up with no other option than to sleep rough. Once they are at that level, it is then all too easy to slip into a form of escape from reality through drink and/or drugs. In many cases, these people are not to be forsaken but to be pitied and, often, just a kind word and some change can completely transform their day – I know because it did for me. Plus, remember karma has a wonderful way of working in unexpected ways.

9. Put a little money away each week – you will always need a "rainy day" fund- Again, from my own experience, running out of cash just as you need it can often put you on the first part of the slippery slope down into even more troubles and create situations that, again, can be difficult to overcome. Try putting aside even a small amount on a regular basis – you will almost certainly need it at some point, if you do, then you will be grateful for your careful saving. When I left home for the first time, if it had not been for my youngest brother, who gave me two £1 coins from his moneybox, I would have left without a penny. It does not matter how small the amount, over a period of time, it will build up and, who knows, one day, you may be really pleased you had done it.

10. Read more books - Reading can be a source of pleasure, it can be relaxing, it can be amusing, it can be educational. The key is to find what type of book gives you pleasure and dig deep. You can gain all kinds of pleasure from reading about other people's experiences, of brave heroes, of tragic disasters, of sporting, political or social heroes, of adventures, real or imaginary.

Over the centuries literally millions of books have been written, despite government (national and local) cutbacks, public libraries still exist in most parts of the country and membership is free. Jump in, dig around and you are almost certain to find something that will open the doorway to a wonderful world of which you might not have dreamed, just waiting for you to sample its delights of its five-star menu.

11. If a jobs worth doing, it's worth doing right. From an early age my mom would say to me "Sean, if a jobs worth doing, then do it well!" This constant reminder from my mom has ingrained into me and remains to this day, even if it's something as mundane as making my bed or hoovering the stairs. I always try and do it well and to the best of my ability; by doing it well I always try and aspire to be the best version of myself I can possibly be. I believe this a great ethos to have in life. It's a simple but effective rule and I try and pass this mantra now onto my children.

12. Listen more and talk less - As the old saying goes, you are the wisest person in the world until you open your mouth and speak...Enough said!

I have tried to work to these little rules or guidelines, as my rule of thumb. They are based upon my own personal experiences and, in many cases, I have learned the hard way. I have learned plenty from my own mistakes, I was going off the rails at an early stage but, at some point, I did get back on them! I was off the rails for quite a long period of my life, but, as I found out, it does get better! My one true relief is that I got it all out of my system early in life.
I think I was always destined for prison, but I am just relieved that I did my time early enough in my life that I can make the most out of the time left. Time is such a valuable commodity, but it does pass too quickly, and you can never go back to live through it all over again.

If you can imagine the scenario, my life has been a bit like arriving at a junction in the path. One path is a short walk to a golden sandy beach, with a load of people walking on it, admiring the gentle warm sea, with the tide lapping at their feet. The second is a steep, sheer mountain face with danger signs which no idiot in his right mind would climb, but which promises the best views ever, all of which will be totally yours, unhindered by anyone else.

I think that you can imagine the track that I would normally take. I hate going down a path that has already been well trodden by a thousand people and who have already seen the view. I like to take the path to a view that not many people have seen. I have always taken the harder, riskier route, which I believed would give me better rewards. You must remember that not all gambles pay off, but you must take the right decision and path for you.

The message from my story is that, no matter how low you sink, no matter how many mistakes you make, there will be a way back or an alternative path that is not quite visible to you because you are not looking for it in the right place. All too often, however, those arms that were put around my shoulders by my family and by Joe and Dave are not available to the majority of those who sink to the bottom of the pile. That is why, whenever I pass someone who is in that situation, it only takes a few seconds for me to remember just what it was like for me when I was sleeping rough on the streets of London, Brussels and Alicante. For these reasons, I always dig into my pocket to see if I have some loose change and, whether I do or not, I always try to offer a few words of kindness and understanding for I knew just how much it meant to me.

While not in any way trying to make a political statement, it is a sad reflection on our 21st century, that there are so many people living rough, abandoned by their families and society in general, some of whom, no doubt would benefit from that same support that my family gave to me. However, just try to remember that, when you are at the bottom of the hole, stop digging! Just stop everything and take a step back, there is always another option!

I hope this book was an enjoyable read, it may hopefully give you a glimpse into my life and the mistakes I've made. I admit I have found it hard at times to continue writing and shelved it a few times because it was difficult to open up a lot of old memories. I hope it may have given you some inspiration. I was in the gutter, so I am talking from experience. There is always a door to be opened, just don't forget that when opportunity knocks, be ready to open the God damn door!

THE END...I very much doubt it!

Printed in Great Britain
by Amazon